THE PAINTING OF
THE LIFE OF ST. FRANCIS
IN ASSISI

THE PAINTING OF

The Life of St. Francis

IN ASSISI

WITH NOTES ON

THE ARENA CHAPEL

AND A 1964 APPENDIX

BY

Leonetto Tintori AND Millard Meiss

The Norton Library
W · W · NORTON & COMPANY · INC ·
NEW YORK

CONTENTS

PREFACE TO THE NORTON LIBRARY EDITION

THIS EDITION differs from its predecessor in only one important respect. It contains in an appendix an article we published in the *Art Bulletin* in 1964; the article adds a number of observations about mural technique that are new but closely related to those in the book. We are thankful to our publisher, W. W. Norton and Company, and particularly to Miss Anne M. Jackson, for recognizing the usefulness of including this article.

A couple of small slips have been corrected in the text, and we have added to the diagrams two lines that were inadvertently omitted. Alastair Smart called attention to these omissions in his review of the book in *The Burlington Magazine*, CV, 1963, pp. 371–375.

L. T.
M. M.

July, 1966

INTRODUCTION

HISTORIANS OF THE ARTS seek answers to certain questions that emerge as they study the evidence – the monuments and objects of the past. During recent times, the questions have been mainly: who, when, and where? From the answers, as discovered or hypothesized, is woven the wide fabric of established history. The question of how a work of art was made has been accorded rather scant notice. To appraise the evidence which relates to this question is not always easy for the scholar trained in art history.

In the following treatise the resources of a distinguished art historian and an equally distinguished and experienced restorer are combined. This combination allowed a thorough exploration and authoritative assessment of the facts about materials and method of construction in a great monument and in others by related workshops. Conclusions were not easily reached, for the conditions are complex and puzzling.

Leonetto Tintori was born in 1908 and went to school in the town of Prato, northwest of Florence and on the Bisenzio. There, later, he enrolled in the Leonardo da Vinci Art School. After he left art school, he worked as a sculptor and developed an interest in the early sculpture of his country. From this he went on to studies in the preservation, repair, and restoration of early wall paintings in fresco. At the end of World War II he was at work in the Camposanto, Pisa, rendering first aid to the frescoes damaged by fire, when he met his present collaborator, who had returned to Italy as the head of the American Committee for the Restoration of Italian Monuments. This committee furnished funds for the detachment of the frescoes and the preparatory drawings, and Tintori devoted himself to the great task of salvage. His present activities lie with works of Giotto. He has cleaned the fresco paintings by that master in the Bardi Chapel at Florence and is at work on those in the Peruzzi Chapel and those in the Arena Chapel at Padua.

Interspersed with these tasks is a series of others at the Capodimonte Museum in Naples. He has been commissioned to study the wall paintings by Piero della Francesca at Arezzo with a view to their conservation.

The coauthor, Millard Meiss, was born in Cincinnati, Ohio, in 1904. He took a Bachelor of Arts degree at Princeton University in 1926 and then studied at Harvard University. He continued his studies in the Graduate School of New York University which granted him the degree, Master of Arts, in 1931, and Doctor of Philosophy in 1933. By that date he had travelled extensively in Europe and was already a lecturer in the history of art. He joined the faculty of Columbia University in 1934 and by 1953 had advanced to the rank of full professor. Harvard University then engaged his services as Professor of Fine Arts and Curator of Paintings in the Fogg Art Museum. Since 1958 he has been Professor of the History of Art in The Institute for Advanced Study, Princeton, New Jersey.

Linkage of the talents, skills, and experience manifest in these two careers in the study of the arts has produced the ensuing treatise. The consequence is a single, firm, and rich gift to all who are concerned. Perhaps, also, their study may stand as a mark of consolidation in the progress of scholarship. It has a strength, surely, that two separate communications could not bring to their readers. Here, in place of any confusing disagreement, is a clear and definite offering, grounded in fact and developed with wise awareness of all the possibilities that could be construed from the factual evidence. It brings answers to most of the questions that can be asked about a work of monumental design, a pictorial drama which will doubtless always be numbered among those few that are venerated as supreme.

George L. Stout
DIRECTOR, Isabella Stewart Gardner Museum, Boston
CHAIRMAN, Board of Consulting Fellows
Conservation Center
Institute of Fine Arts, New York University

FOREWORD

LE OSSERVAZIONI TECNICHE che Millard Meiss e Leonetto Tintori hanno fatto, con esame attento e minuzioso, sul ciclo giottesco di Assisi, costituiscono, forse, il primo esempio di collaborazione, a scopo scientifico, tra studiosi e restauratori; e questa collaborazione, qualora venga condotta con tecnici che siano del tutto svincolati dalla vecchia empirica pratica del restauro, ancor oggi purtroppo largamente seguita e, spesso, lodata dal pubblico, potrà certamente dare notevoli e imprevisti risultati per gli studi di storia dell'arte.

Già diversi anni fa era occorso, a chi scrive queste brevi note, di richiamare l'attenzione sul fatto che in un affresco può esser stabilito, e accertato con assoluta sicurezza, non solo quali e quante siano le varie giornate – o meglio riprese – di lavoro, ma anche il loro progressivo susseguirsi nel tempo; e questo per il fatto che l'intonaco delle successive riprese viene necessariamente a sormontare in parte, se pure alle volte in maniera quasi impercettibile, l'intonaco precedente, lungo la linea in cui con quello si trova a combaciare. Questa osservazione – che pur può avere notevole interesse per conoscere lo svolgersi creativo e lo sviluppo dell'opera d'arte – non è però la sola, né la più importante, che possa esser fatta, sempre dal lato tecnico, sugli affreschi; se si ricordi, infatti, che il Cennini, nel suo famoso e per noi preziosissimo "Libro dell'Arte," ci fa sapere che gli antichi artisti, per avere un risultato perfetto secondo il proprio intendimento, si preparavano da loro stessi l'intonaco, su cui avrebbero subito dopo dato vita alle pitture murali, verrà per noi logica la conclusione che si dovranno avere – come per qualsiasi opera fatta da uomo – diversità negli intonaci eseguiti da mani differenti; mentre, di conseguenza, anche in questa umile fatica manuale, si ritroveranno, per ogni pittore, particolarità proprie, che saranno identiche qualora si tratti – come nel caso di un grande ciclo di affreschi – di opere eseguite in un ristretto lasso di tempo. Si potranno così notare uguaglianze o differenze nella composizione stessa della calcina, per diversa proporzione tra calce e rena; oppure l'intonaco potrà esser più o meno levigato; o vi saranno diversità nelle attaccature delle varie riprese di lavoro, e così via.

Passando poi all'esame della pittura stessa, l'uso dei colori — come è logico e come ce ne dà prova la lettura delle pagine del Cennini — lasciava liberi gli artisti di seguire, nella comune tecnica, varietà di metodi. Innumerevoli quindi potranno essere le osservazioni anche in questo campo; e tutte queste osservazioni, se ben vagliate, potranno costituire un complesso di conoscenze tecniche veramente notevole.

E' da auspicare quindi che l'esame condotto ora sul grande ciclo assisiate, con particolare amore, con rigoroso metodo e con investigazione minuziosa e scevra di preconcetti, possa essere esteso ad altri complessi di pitture murali, per poter apprestare, con appassionata ricerca, elementi nuovi al progredire degli studi di storia dell'arte.

Ugo Procacci
Soprintendente ai Monumenti, Firenze

PREFACE

AIDED BY BETTER PHOTOGRAPHS and an advancing knowledge of early Italian painting as a whole, we have learned much in recent years about the chronology and authorship of the frescoes in the Upper Church at Assisi. Our judgment that they disclose a crucial stage in the history of Western painting has been strengthened. Only a historian who lacks perspective on his own work or the work of his time would however maintain that we have attained to the full truth about these paintings, or that the constant searching study of them during the past sixty years will not continue in the next sixty. Since all contemporary local records of these primordial monuments of the *stil nuovo* have been lost, and no unequivocal statements about any part of them were recorded before Vasari's *Lives* two and a half centuries later, scholarship is bound to persevere in its inquiry, from one point of view or another.

The present book offers both much less and a little more than most contributions to the subject. Less because it does not attempt conclusions about the great problem of the participation of Giotto — though relevant observations are scattered through the text — and more because it presents a new order of facts about the *Legend of St. Francis*. These facts are direct objects of experience. This does not imply of course that they are free of error, though we believe it does not rise above five percent. And they are, in any event, subject to control by other investigators, possessed of course of the requisite experience and armed with some simple equipment. It is possible, furthermore, to predict the places at which the likelihood of error is greater; they will be pointed out in the course of the discussion.

Our primary procedure is a venture into what may be called mural topography. We have located and mapped the sutures in the intonaco of the frescoes. By examination of the structure of the intonaco at these sutures we have determined, sometimes with difficulty but almost always with certainty, the sequence in which the adjacent areas of intonaco were laid. Observation of these features of the surface enables us, first of all, to settle a question that has been discussed for a long time: the sequence of the execution of the twenty-eight frescoes of the cycle. Within each fresco, furthermore, we have demarcated the areas that were painted at one time — usually during one day, extending perhaps in very damp weather to two days. The order of execution of these sections or patches within each scene is also determined, though at certain stages it is impossible to choose between two alternatives. A few of these alternative sequences are pointed out in the text. They complicate but do not block our insight into the production of each fresco from the first day's work to the last.

Each section representing a day's work was normally frescoed by one painter. True, in large sections an assistant may have worked alongside, taking over the flat surfaces of architecture or the blue background or the ornament of drapery. But the delineation of the divisions of a fresco is clearly relevant to the larger aspects of collaboration within each fresco and in the cycle as a whole. The publication of the patterns has thus a certain timeliness, because recent criticism has moved away from the old monolithic conception of the frescoes, and has sought to explain many of the stylistic difficulties that they present by hypotheses of collaboration. These hypotheses must now conform to the structure presented in the following pages. We hope at the same time that this structure will in turn stimulate fresh observations and disclose aspects of the paintings that have hitherto been overlooked.

We have ourselves refrained from extensive excursions into the realm of style. We have preferred to present our findings primarily as instruments for the renewed study of problems of authorship, unencumbered with much speculation of our own. We have, however, constantly pointed to the light that procedures and techniques cast on questions of this sort. In some instances — the later date of the first fresco in the cycle, for example — our findings bring controversy to an end, while proving the correctness of the majority opinion. Even where, however, our evidence conforms to the usual judgment we do not regard its publication as supererogatory. On the contrary, since judgments of style can seldom be proved absolutely, opportunities to do so are important as validations of a method.

The kind of topographical investigation that we have undertaken is not novel. Many conservators and historians, especially since the end of the war, have paid attention to the sutures in the intonaco of fresco paintings, at least here and there, and have become aware of their significance for the history of art. But the study of them on so large and comprehensive a scale has not previously been undertaken, nor perhaps on so unpromising a surface. Indeed it is only fifteen years ago that Professor Pietro Toesca, author of a monograph on Giotto and the supervisor of a great photographic campaign in the Upper Church which brought him close to the surface of the *Legend*, said that very few joints could be detected. Unlike the intonaco employed by Raphael and Michelangelo, Professor Toesca added, that at Assisi was too thin to reveal the pattern of the successive days' work.[1]

The possibility of mapping the successive stages in the execution of the *Legend of St. Francis* derives from a knowledge of fresco technique that has increased greatly during the past twenty years. This advance was promoted, it must be confessed, by the war. As in fields such as surgery, the emergency accelerated the trial of novel techniques of conservation, occasionally at risks greater than normal. But once the worst ravages of the war were repaired those responsible for conservation, especially in Tuscany, recognized that they were faced with an emergency of another kind. The rate of deterioration of many murals seemed to have increased alarmingly in recent years, and in most cases the only way to avoid complete ruin was to detach the paintings from the walls. This great campaign to salvage Florentine frescoes, directed by Professor Ugo Procacci, was accompanied by unprecedented advances in our knowledge of the technique and art of mural painting.

Until recently we knew very much less about painting on the wall than about painting on panel or canvas. There was not even a clear conception of the distinction between painting *ad affresco* and painting *a secco*. Indeed, the cycle that is the subject of this book was said in 1923 to have been painted entirely *a secco*.[2] And what appears to us in these paintings to be preparatory drawing on the intonaco, visible where the colors have flaked off, was declared only a few years ago to be drawing on the *arriccio*, exposed by loss of the intonaco.[3] Time and again, until quite recently, the frescoes of the life of St. Francis were described as defaced by repaint.[4] Apart however from the large patches where the intonaco has fallen away — those within the scenes indicated in the reproductions of this book — and the retouching of many very small losses, they appear to us remarkably free of repainting.

Up to twenty years ago, before the appearance of important studies by Ugo Procacci, Robert Oertel, and Eve Borsook, our knowledge of mural technique derived more from books than from examination of the surviving monuments. Our views were still essentially those of Cennino Cennini and Vasari; and under the influence of their strong preference for true fresco we overestimated the extent of it. Everyone has been aware that certain colors, such as azurite, could not be utilized in a water medium, but we have learned in recent years that true fresco painting is often greatly "adulterated," for convenience or other reasons. Even major cycles, alas, such as Giotto's in the Peruzzi Chapel, contain scarcely any fresco at all but are almost entirely in the more perishable tempera.

Twenty years ago very few if any students knew, and some still do not know, precisely what they are looking at in a late thirteenth- or fourteenth-century mural. We recognize total destruction, but we are not equally certain whether, in a given area, we see the finished painting or only a stage in the preparation of the finished painting, the final film having vanished in great part or entirely. Professor Toesca, in the introduction to the very valuable corpus of photographs mentioned above, referred to a few of these larger losses in the St. Francis cycle.[5] We have believed it useful to record all *major* alterations of the original surface — at least all those of which we are aware. These alterations are due chiefly to the disintegration or exfoliation of pigments applied *a secco*. We have noted also some alterations due to chemical changes, such as the common blackening of lead white or the transformation of azurite blue into malachite green. Both these changes have affected considerably the appearance of the frescoes. We should have preferred to carry much further the description of the alteration of colors, especially of the unstable greens. But to accomplish that we would have had to identify all the pigments by laboratory analysis and we would have needed the collaboration of a qualified chemist. This large enterprise was not practical then, and it would in any event have postponed publication for some time of the observations already made. Identification of the pigments of frescoes and their chemical vicissitudes is urgently needed, and we hope it will be undertaken systematically in Italy soon under official auspices.

An unexpected result of our examination of the frescoes was the discovery, in the Arena Chapel, of significant changes made by Giotto during the course of the work.

We are grateful to Padre Giuseppe Zaccaria, prior of S. Francesco and Ispettore Onorario, for permission to spend long days in the church on two separate occasions. Like many other students we are beneficiaries of his affection for the church and its paintings, and his deep concern for their conservation. George L. Stout was always ready to draw on his incomparable technical knowledge for our benefit. Ingrid Linderos has our warmest thanks for the skill and care with which she prepared the diagrams in the book, Deirdre Roskill for her faultless typescript, and Edith W. Kirsch for her equally accurate work on the index. We are indebted to Dr. Francesco Valcanover for several photographs of the frescoes in the Arena Chapel made before the recent cleaning. The Institute for Advanced Study in Princeton, and its director, J. Robert Oppenheimer, have generously promoted the enterprise in various ways.

Despite the ocean that normally separates us we contrived to prepare much of this book together. Leonetto Tintori of course took the lead in the exploration of technical problems, but we worked side by side on the scaffolds, except for the study of sutures in the houses at Pompeii and around the shafts in Assisi, which Leonetto Tintori had to carry on alone. The writing is due to Millard Meiss, but fortunately Tintori was able to join him in Princeton while the final draft was prepared.

We are thankful for help of all kinds gaily given by our wives. While we worked in the cold church we often — we must confess — envied their collaboration in the sun outside, checking our drawings, ambling to the electrician or the stationer, or discovering endlessly new aspects of the wonderful view.

Leonetto Tintori
Millard Meiss

March 10, 1961

NOTES

1. *Gli affreschi della Vita di San Francesco nella Chiesa Superiore del Santuario di Assisi, Artis Monumenta Photographice Edita*, III, Florence, (1946), p. 13.

2. Crowe and Cavalcaselle, *A History of Painting in Italy*, ed. L. Douglas, London, 1923, II, p. 13 note 3.

3. Toesca, *loc. cit.*

4. Douglas, in Crowe and Cavalcaselle, *op. cit.*, II, p. 18 note 2.

CHAPTER I

On Mural Technique

THE mural techniques employed in Italy in the late thirteenth and fourteenth centuries, described in detail in Cennino Cennini's *Libro dell'Arte*, have ancient origins. Both true fresco (i.e., painting with a water vehicle on wet lime plaster) and various kinds of secco painting (i.e., painting on dry plaster) were practiced as early as Mycenaean times.[1] These techniques were continued in the Greco-Roman period, and there are references to them in Roman texts. Vitruvius describes the application of three coats of powdered marble to the wall, each coat progressively finer in texture, and then adds:

After they are rendered solid by the use of the plasterer's tools and polished to the whiteness of marble, they will show a glittering splendor when the colors are laid on with the last coat. When the colors are carefully laid upon the wet plaster, they do not fail but are permanently durable, because the lime has its moisture removed in the kilns, and becoming attenuated and porous, is compelled by its dryness to seize upon whatever happens to present itself.[2]

Vitruvius gives a physical explanation of the durability of fresco, whereas this important characteristic is due essentially to a chemical process, the carbonation of the lime, in the course of which the pigments are bound into the solid crystalline mass of the plaster.[3] Pliny too was impressed by the solidity and durability of painting on plaster. He speaks admiringly of the survival of a mural that may well have been true fresco. Representing nude figures of Atalanta and Helena, this painting was not damaged by the collapse of the temple in which it was later found, and it even resisted the aggressive attentions of a Roman emperor. Pliny says, "The Emperor Caligula

1l. Roman, first century, B.C., *Dionysiac Mysteries* (detail). Pompeii, *Villa dei Mister*

4

r. Roman, first century, B.C., *Dionysiac Mysteries* (detail). Pompeii, *Villa dei Misteri.*

from lustful motives attempted to remove them, but the consistency of the plaster would not allow this to be done."[4]

When discussing pigments Pliny lists several which want a dry plaster and, unlike those he had enumerated previously, cannot be applied in a water vehicle or to a wet surface: "Ex omnibus coloribus cretulam amant udoque inlini recusant purpurissum, Indicum, caeruleum, Melinum, auripigmentum, Appianum, cerussa." "Of all the colors those which love a dry surface of white clay, and refuse to be applied to a damp plaster, are purple, indigo, blue, Melian, orpiment, Appian and ceruse."[5] Insofar as a few colors require a nonaqueous vehicle (egg or another organic substance) on a dry surface true fresco was then, as always, a somewhat mixed technique. But there remains a crucial distinction between true fresco and other techniques that may conveniently be grouped together as secco: in the latter the process of carbonation is completed before the paint is applied. Whether or not the plaster is moistened again is irrelevant.

The statements of Vitruvius testify to the use in his time of fresco as well as secco methods. Most recent opinion, however, holds that extant Roman murals are largely or exclusively secco, and that if true fresco is used at all, it is limited to the ground color.[6] Physical or chemical analysis has commonly been employed in the search for the presence of an organic binder, which would identify one of the secco methods. Organic substances might, however, be present accidentally, or they might have been applied later to the surface of the painting.[7] It is true that a cursory examination of the surface of paintings in Pompeian houses discloses most frequently the straight sutures of the *pontate*, or large rectangles of intonaco, characteristic of secco painting. There are, however, occasional sutures, in the *Sala degli Elefanti* of the *Casa dello Scheletro* for example, of the kind that, in our opinion, indicate a true fresco technique. A close study of one cycle of paintings, outstanding for its quality, proves, we believe, that the figures were executed in true fresco. The sutures in the paintings in the *Villa dei Misteri* are very fine but nevertheless discoverable (Figs. 1*l* and 1*r*). They commonly follow the outlines of the figures, and it is impossible to imagine the usefulness of so intricate a scheme of plastering except for the application of the colors on moist lime. The pattern of patches is, furthermore, essentially identical with those appearing in Trecento paintings that, for many other reasons, are identifiable as true frescoes. In one of the finest figure-compositions, then, that has come down to us from Roman times the technique appears to be basically fresco.[8]

The history of mural technique in the Middle Ages remains to be written. Between the two poles of pure fresco and pure secco a variety of procedures was employed. The *Hermeneia* of Mount Athos, a late text reflecting eleventh- and twelfth-century techniques, recommends painting as much as possible on wet intonaco, and then proceeding, with a modified vehicle, on the dry plaster.[9] It seems probable that the method known in antiquity and characterized in modern times by the paradoxical but useful term "fresco secco" was widely employed. In fresco secco the vehicle is lime water, as often in true fresco, but the paint is applied to a plaster that, though freshly moistened for the occasion, has previously dried. This technique, described in the eleventh-century treatise of Theophilus,[10] is a compromise, and like most compromises, not highly successful, at least from the viewpoint of durability. For the process of carbonation was completed before the paint was applied; and though the addition of lime to the water produced a thin crust of lime and color, the adhesion of this crust to the plaster is not comparable to the incorporation of the pigments in true fresco.

Fresco secco and tempera were commonly practiced in the Middle Ages. True fresco, it seems, was rare. It began, however, to replace the established techniques in the late thirteenth century, and specifically in Rome, if the thesis of Robert Oertel's important study is correct.[11] If the change did indeed occur principally in Rome this city would have made a major contribution to the *stil nuovo* in the sphere of technique as well as style. Indeed the inspiration for both may have come from the same source, because some of the Early Christian or even ancient mural paintings that so deeply impressed Cavallini and his colleagues may have been executed in fresco technique. And Cavallini would have had an opportunity to study an Early Christian technique closely on at least one occasion, when he restored and enlarged the fifth-century mural cycle in the nave of

S. Paolo fuori le mura (Fig. 73, p. 188). Once again, then, fateful technical and stylistic innovations might have been born together.

The appearance and development of the new technique may be observed in the Upper Church in Assisi, painted by Roman masters and by Florentines who had had extensive experience in the papal city. The technical shift can be discerned in the topography of the paintings. In secco technique the uppermost layer of fine plaster (intonaco) that will receive the paint is spread in broad bands, the size of which is normally determined by the area that the plasterer and the painter could conveniently cover while working on one platform of a scaffold. For such an area the Italian language has a word, *pontata*, derived from *ponte* or stage of a scaffold. In Cimabue's frescoes the intonaco was applied in these large bands, extending as usual the width of the scene and as high as a man could conveniently reach.[12] In the fresco of the *Crucifixion* the lower edge of what is probably the middle *pontata* is clearly visible, passing just above the knees of the standing figures and above the head of the kneeling St. Francis (Fig. 2).

In these large areas only some of the outlines could be laid — in this case in a yellow color — while the plaster was still wet.[13] The rest was executed *a secco*, and to this technique must be ascribed part of the cause of the ruinous state of the frescoes. The deterioration was promoted by moisture, constantly seeping through the stone and through an unusually thin coat of rough plaster or *arriccio*.[14] White lead, furthermore, was used extensively, and it has turned black. Where the intonaco was spread directly on a large stone in a small rectangle immediately over the door in the lower right-hand corner of the *Crucifixion* the white lead has not darkened (Fig. 2a).[15] Blues and greens without lead are, however, not well preserved in this rectangle, so that the causes of deterioration in Cimabue's cycle are evidently complex. The colors are unchanged in parts of the vaults and of the angels in the arcades above the scenes, perhaps because the areas are smaller and proportionately more was painted while the intonaco was damp. There is also a precious specimen of Cimabue's finished surface in the apostle seated last at the right in the *Death of the Virgin*. It is a small patch of soft,

2. Cimabue, *Crucifixion*. Assisi, S. Francesco. *Pontata*.

2*a*. Cimabue, *Crucifixion*
Assisi, (detail).
S. Francesco.

3. Roman painter, *The Building of the Ark*. Assisi, S. Francesco. *Pontata*.

4. Roman painter,
Creation of Eve.
Assisi, S. Francesco.
Pontata.

luminous gray drapery, and because it is rather square in shape it may well have been painted on a *freshly laid* patch of plaster that filled a hole left by a beam of the scaffold or some other object.

The division into *pontate*, as in Cimabue's frescoes, is visible in the better preserved scenes in the two bays nearest the transepts, particularly in the scenes of the Old Testament on the north wall, such as *The Building of the Ark* (Fig. 3) or the *Creation of Eve* (Fig. 4).[16] The technique and the pigments employed in these frescoes are, however, somewhat different from Cimabue's and the color has resisted moisture far more successfully. But the decisive innovations in Assisi occur in the paintings in the third and fourth bays, especially in the Isaac scenes and the *Lamentation*, which are often nowadays attributed to the youthful Giotto and are certainly the most advanced works at the upper level in the church. The style of these paintings is related to Cavallini, and indeed the surface of Cavallini's paintings in S. Cecilia is divided, not into *pontate*, but irregular *giornate* or areas paintable in one day — clear indication of the use of true fresco.[17]

In the one fresco of this group in Assisi that we were able to examine at close range, the *Lamentation*, or at least the right half of it, the joints of the *giornate* were distinctly visible. The raking light disclosed also incisions in the plaster of the haloes, made no doubt, as usually, to avoid loss of the outline of the head in the process of gilding. We were surprised to discover, in addition to these incisions, numerous others in the intonaco (Fig. 5). These incised lines are in the draperies of the figures, outlining them or defining folds. They vary in length; some are only about six inches long, others as much as four or five feet. They vary somewhat in depth also; the deepest, in the drapery of the figure standing at the extreme right, must have been traced when the plaster was very wet and soft.

What is the significance of these incisions? Others have been reported recently: in a late thirteenth-century fresco of a saint in S. Bartolommeo in Pantano, Pistoia, and in the draperies in the early fourteenth-century paintings of mixed technique in the Kariye Camii in Constantinople.[18] They were employed, of course, as a salient kind of drawing to define the draperies and the folds. Two

5. Giotto (?), *Lamentation of Christ* (detail). Assisi, S. Francesco. Incisions in intonaco.

aspects of their use in the Assisi *Lamentation* are noteworthy. They are not confined to areas which are to be overlaid with a heavy opaque paint, such as azurite, that would conceal an underdrawing simply "drawn" or painted on the surface. They are, on the contrary, numerous in the pale rose drapery of the figure at the extreme right. In the second place, whereas the incisions in the aureoles appear to have the small irregularities of lines drawn freehand, many of those in the drapery seem to be invariable in width and depth and regular in their curvature, like those impressed from a full-scale model.[19]

The use of cartoons of any kind, however, has not been observed in murals painted before the middle of the fifteenth century, at least as far as the figures are concerned. We can detect their use at that time from their effect on the intonaco; the cartoons themselves, on perishable paper, have not survived. Around the mid-fifteenth century the *spolvero*, a process of transferring to the wall (or to a panel) the lines of a cartoon by dusting pigment through perforations in them (Fig. 6), began to be employed for figures, as in frescoes by Domenico Veneziano in S. Croce and Castagno in S. Apollonia.[20] This method was known a hundred years earlier, however, and used for decorative forms, in the borders of Orcagna's frescoes in S. M. Novella and S. Croce.[21] The cartoon as we normally understand it — a full-scale drawing on heavy paper (*cartone*), the lines of which are to be transferred by the pressure of a stylus — began to replace the *spolvero* only at the end of the fifteenth century. It would certainly be premature to suggest that the incisions in the *Lamentation* around 1292–1293 imply the use of a cartoon, but the question, which is interesting, must be raised. Eventually it will be answered by closer study of the entire surface of this fresco and of others of this period, though transfer by incision will not prove to have been frequent.

In his craftsman's handbook, written probably soon after 1400, Cennino Cennini describes the stages in the execution of a fresco that he believed were normal in the work of Giotto and his followers. This text is very well known, but it may be useful to quote the passages most relevant to the discussion and diagrams that follow.

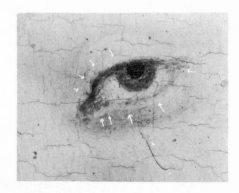

6. Domenico Veneziano,
Eye of Christ, detail of
Madonna. Washington,
National Gallery.
Spolvero.

When you want to work on a wall, which is the most agreeable and impressive kind of work, first of all get some lime and some sand, each of them well sifted. . . . And wet them up well with water; and wet up enough to last you for two or three weeks. And let it stand for a day or so, until the heat goes out of it: for when it is hot, the plaster which you put on cracks afterward. When you are ready to plaster, first sweep the wall well, and wet it down thoroughly, for you cannot get it too wet. And take your lime mortar, well worked over, a trowelful at a time; and plaster once or twice, to begin with, to get the plaster flat on the wall. Then, when you want to work, remember first to make this plaster quite uneven and fairly rough. Then when the plaster is dry, take the charcoal, and draw and compose according to the scene or figures which you have to do; and take all your measurements carefully. . . . Then compose the scenes or figures with charcoal, as I have described. . . . Then take a small, pointed bristle brush, and a little ocher without tempera, as thin as water; and proceed to copy and draw in your figures, shading as you did with washes when you were learning to draw. Then take a bunch of feathers, and sweep the drawing free of the charcoal.

Then take a little sinoper without tempera, and with a fine pointed brush proceed to mark out noses, eyes, the hair, and all the accents and outlines of the figures; and see to it that these figures are properly adjusted in all their dimensions, for these give you a chance to know and allow for the figures which you have to paint . . . and when you are ready, take some of the aforesaid lime mortar, well worked over with spade and trowel, successively, so that it seems like an ointment. Then consider in your own mind how much work you can do in a day; for whatever you plaster you ought to finish up. It is true that sometimes in winter, in damp weather, working on a stone wall, the plaster will occasionally keep fresh until the next day; but do not delay if you can help it, because working on the fresh plaster, that is, that day's, is the strongest tempera and the best and the most delightful kind of work. So then, plaster a section with plaster, fairly thin, but not excessively, and quite even; first wetting down the old plaster. Then take your large bristle brush in your hand; dip it in clear water; beat it, and sprinkle over your plaster. And with a little block the size of the palm of your hand, proceed to rub with a circular motion over the surface of the well-moistened plaster, so that the little block may succeed in removing mortar wherever there is not enough, and in evening up your plaster nicely. Then wet the plaster with that brush, if you need to; and rub over the plaster with the point of your trowel, very straight and clean. Then snap your lines in the same system and dimensions which you adopted previously on the plaster underneath.

And let us suppose that in a day you have just one head to do, a youthful saint's, like Our Most Holy Lady's. . . .[22]

Then Cennino proceeds to describe in detail this day's work, having selected as a model a head, the form in which Trecento expressiveness ordinarily culminates. The sinopia drawing of the head has, of course, been covered by the intonaco, so the painter begins by outlining the head once again, in a mixture of dark ocher, black, lime white, and *cinabrese* that was known as *verdaccio* in Florence and *bazzèo* in Siena. The *verdaccio* drawing of the head and the features is then shaded in green earth or terra verde. From this point on, Cennino says, practice varies somewhat, but the best procedure is to touch in the lips and cheeks with rose and then model the flesh, using for the purpose a pink of three values. At the end the accents, white or black, are laid into eyes and nose, and the hair is executed in similar stages.

The procedure of painting a head is paradigmatic; though the pigments vary, the painting of other forms follows the same stages. Like Pliny, Cennino enumerates the pigments that cannot be mixed with water. Some are identical in the two lists. Their vehicle usually was egg. They are heightened by white lead or, better, *giallorino* rather than lime white, and they are applied after the plaster has dried. Though some of these pigments, such as azurite, were very prominent in Trecento "frescoes," as Cennino knew well, the essential and proper technique for the wall consisted of an aqueous vehicle on a damp intonaco.

All of this was, Cennino pointed out, the technique of "Giotto the great master" and his followers. That, for him, settled the matter; no other techniques, even if familiar to him, would have been worth describing. In recent years, however, observations facilitated by the campaign to conserve frescoes have raised questions about the universality of "Giotto's technique," and, worse still, about its employment by the grand old master himself. For one thing we know that in two of the three fresco cycles commonly accepted as his, Giotto did not use sinopia drawings. Small traces of drawing on the intonaco of the Arena Chapel suggest the presence of sinopias there, but they are not visible in any of the places where the intonaco has fallen away in the Bardi Chapel. There certainly were no such drawings in the Peruzzi Chapel, for reasons that will become apparent in a moment. Here, of course, as in the case of other mural paintings, the wall itself may have been employed for preliminary study. Indeed, in the Arena Chapel there are fragments of red earth drawings on the chancel arch. Some of these lines may be seen on the whitened bricks near the house of the Annunciate Virgin, while a red arc is drawn on the stone, curving from the right hand of God (on a panel) down towards the central lion-head on the base of the throne. Inasmuch as such drawings were covered by the *arriccio* they were considerably removed in time from the process of painting, and they were therefore much less effective than sinopias as guides for the painting.

Sinopia drawings have not been discovered in the *Legend of St. Francis* in Assisi nor in Simone Martini's cycle in the same church, though here the *arriccio* is so thin that it has not yet been possible to expose its surface when detaching the fresco. More decisively in conflict with Cennino's prescriptions is the fact that the amount of secco painting in the Bardi Chapel exceeds what he recommended. The reasons for its use often were, as far as we can see, not its superior aesthetic effect, and certainly not its durability, but its practical advantages, freeing the painter from the tyranny of the drying patch of intonaco and permitting interruptions of the work as well as, on the whole, greater speed of execution. Worst of all as far as Cennino is concerned, the Peruzzi Chapel was painted almost entirely on once dried intonaco (Fig. 72, p. 183).

Though awareness of the secco technique of the Peruzzi Chapel would have been disturbing to Cennino, to Vasari it would have come as a great shock. The use of secco increased during the fifteenth century, and by the time Vasari began to write his chapters on technique, true fresco, once the accepted (but not at all sole) technique, required defense and championship.[23] It is sanctioned by tradition, he says; it was much used by the *antichi* and also by the *vecchi moderni* (the era of Giotto). It is the most beautiful, surpassing oil and all other pictorial techniques. And it is the most durable — indeed his warm praise on this score seems a little sanguine today.[24] The values of the mid-sixteenth century become more evident when he adds that it is the fastest, requiring the completion in one day of what in other techniques might be done in several. Only a well-trained, resolute, and rapid hand, subject to a firm, comprehensive judgment, can succeed in it. Whence painters successful in other techniques often fail in this.[25] It is, indeed, the most difficult because, in addition to the requirements of assurance and speed, the final effect of the colors must be anticipated. The wall when damp shows colors that, when dry, are no longer the same.

In this remarkable passage, the most enthusiastic and brilliant ever written about true fresco, Vasari does not descend to details of procedure. In one important respect the procedure in true fresco in his own day differed from that of the fourteenth century, and he refers to this difference in his Life of Simone Martini, or Memmi as he called him. When writing of a work that he ascribes to this painter in the refectory of the monastery of Assisi, he describes it as incomplete, and indeed not carried beyond the red earth drawing on the *arriccio*. Other visible specimens of this kind of drawing are, he says, the consequence not of incompleteness but of the exfoliation of the intonaco. Now these drawings were to the old masters, Vasari adds, what the cartoon is to us.[26]

The difference between the two procedures, between the sinopia of the fourteenth and fifteenth centuries and the cartoon (at first *spolvero*) of the later fifteenth and sixteenth centuries, corresponds to a basic stylistic difference between the two periods. The rapid drawing and painting of a complex form on the intonaco guided simply by a memory of the preparatory drawing was appropriate only to an era in which forms were relatively conventional. All heads, for instance, approximated canons to such a degree that the variables were readily remembered, or quickly invented by the painter as, during the allotted day, he executed the work. Nothing is a more accurate barometer of the increasing individuality, life-likeness, and therefore uniqueness of forms than the introduction of the *spolvero* in the fifteenth century. Though this kind of cartoon was, as we have remarked, employed for decorative forms by Orcagna, its function in this case was no doubt to facilitate repetition of the same pattern. But, from the mid-fifteenth century on, the purpose of the *spolvero*, and later the cartoon proper, was to fix not the repetitive but the unique. It was intended to transfer quickly to the wet intonaco the outlines of a particular form that was the final product of previous contemplation and development.

The efficacy of the cartoon is clear enough, but that of the sinopia raises some questions. In the earlier Middle Ages pictorial forms were considerably less variable than those of the Trecento, yet the preparatory drawing was normally on the intonaco, and therefore remained a quite visible framework for the painting. Why, as the individuality of forms increased in the late Dugento and early Trecento, was the drawing relegated to a layer that was concealed at the time of painting? The peculiarities of true fresco were certainly largely responsible. Since, for one thing, fresco painting was done in relatively small patches, often containing no more than a single head, the entire figure or the entire composition had to be drawn elsewhere, on a space of adequate size. In the second place fresco required such speed of execution that, once the intonaco was spread, very little time could be given to a preparatory drawing. Of the daylight hours available for each patch, the fewer hours, or indeed minutes, given to the drawing, the more remained for the painting.

It was the nature of fresco, then, that exacted sacrifices of the preparatory drawing. Its special requirements led painters of the late thirteenth century to adopt a procedure that had long been current, not in painting as such but in mosaic, where the forms were drawn on the setting bed of the cubes.[27] Trecento painters evidently judged that the advantages of fresco outweighed the complication of the process of drawing. The new technique, however, probably brought some gains as well as losses even with regard to drawing. Alterations of a drawing on the intonaco are more troublesome than on the *arriccio*, where they would of course be concealed. And if these alterations, after some contemplation, were to be extensive, it was far simpler to erase on the *arriccio* or to replaster, as Traini often did in the Camposanto,[28] than to cut out and replace the intonaco.

We can readily understand, then, that the preparation of a fresco by drawing on the intonaco only would not have been practical. In these circumstances, then, why were cartoons not introduced? They were employed by Orcagna for ornament, as we have remarked, and Cennino describes the use of the *spolvero* when designing panels. One or two possible instances before 1400 of the use of cartoons for figures have been observed, but it seems unlikely that they will ever be proved common. Vasari points out that the drawings on the *arriccio* served "the old masters" as cartoons did their successors: "il quale modo di fare era il cartone che i nostri maestri vecchi facevano, per lavorare in fresco per maggior brevità. . . ."[29] It is not clear whether the "modelli" described by Alberti are inscribed with parallel lines for transfer to the *arriccio* or the intonaco; but we do know that Masaccio employed a grid for the Madonna's head on the intonaco of the *Trinity*.[30] Perhaps the relatively high cost of paper is largely responsible for the rarity of large cartoons until the mid-fifteenth century, although a real demand for them might have been met by cloth or some similar material which could be reused. There is, in fact, no way of ascertaining that Trecento painters felt the need of prior full-scale drawings of their figures.

In Cennino Cennini's account of fresco procedure the painter first "composes" ("disegnia e compone") on the *arriccio*, employing charcoal, and then elaborates and fixes this drawing by the use of ocher and subsequently sinopia. When later in the treatise Cennino describes the stages of painting on panel, which begin likewise with a drawing in charcoal on the gesso, he speaks of correcting the lines when desirable by erasure of the charcoal, and then he adds: "When you have finished drawing your figure, especially if it is a very valuable ancona, so that you are counting on profit and reputation from it, leave it alone for a few days, going back to it now and then to look it over and improve it wherever it still needs something."[31]

Curiously there are no references to alterations of the drawing in the earlier passage on fresco, though one would expect them to be more frequent in a large area than in a much smaller one. This would be true especially if the drawings on the *arriccio* were the first record of the composition, unprepared by a prior study elsewhere on smaller scale.

Is it possible, despite Cennino's silence, that compositions were first drawn in small scale on a tablet or on parchment or even on paper, rather than emerging originally full-blown on the wall? Until recently it was assumed that Trecento painters often made preparatory drawings before approaching the wall.[32] Some years ago Robert Oertel in a thorough and comprehensive study concluded that they seldom did, but his argument, while dealing with the problem historically for the first time, is not entirely convincing. Oertel rests his case to a large extent on his belief that Trecento painters could not envisage a large fresco in a small drawing. The monumental qualities of painting, especially of Giottesque painting, he says, could not be conveyed in greatly reduced scale.[33] Actual size is of course relevant to artistic conception. It is bound up with the effect of works of art generally, but we think it would be difficult to prove that it is so much more essential to the Trecento that the main elements of a mural could not be imagined and recorded in diminutive scale. Haven't we, in fact, evidence that the opposite is the case? We shall shortly, on p. 34, refer to quite incontrovertible instances of the reuse of fresco compositions and figures at reduced scale in comparatively small altarpieces. There is little basic difference of character between Taddeo Gaddi's frescoes of the Annunciation, Nativity, or the Adoration of the Magi and his representations of these subjects on panels, including small predellas such as the *Nativity* in Dijon, or pinnacles, such as the *Annunciation* in the Pistoia altarpiece.[34] If, in a photograph, the cusped frame of Daddi's small predella of the *Meeting at the Golden Gate* in the Uffizi is masked,[35] who would feel certain of its actual size?

In support of his thesis, Oertel refers to the rarity of drawings that could have served as preliminary records of fresco compositions. Such drawings are indeed rare now, but we shall try to show that originally they were not uncommon. It is important to remember that very few Trecento drawings of any kind whatever have been preserved. What is significant, therefore, is not the absolute number of such drawings but their proportion to the total number surviving. Surely most of the drawings of this period have been lost. The appreciation of them as works of art developed only later, and there were no collectors to preserve them after their usefulness in the workshops ended.

While the cost of paper for full-size cartoons would have been high, it apparently was not a limiting factor in small sizes. Paper imported by Arabs was employed for documents in Italy in the early thirteenth century. Two mills for the production of paper were operating in 1283, and in the fourteenth century manufacture spread from Fabriano to Colle di Val d'Elsa, Bologna, Forlì, Parma, Padua, and Treviso. In 1330 there were twenty mills in Fabriano alone. By this time Italy was the center for paper production in the West, and large quantities were exported to France and Germany, where mills were established only after 1390. One manufacturer of Fabriano alone shipped from the port of Talamone 55,000 pounds of paper (240 bales) in 3½ years. In 1382 paper is said to have cost only one-sixth as much as parchment. In Bologna, as elsewhere, the quality and price of paper were municipally controlled. In 1389 the price of a pound of paper was fixed at ⅛ of a lira, equal to about ¹⁄₂₀ of a Florentine florin. At this time a painter would receive at least 70 or 80 florins for the painting of an altarpiece.[36] In the fourteenth century, then, paper in small sizes would seem to have been economically available to painters, and it is not surprising that Cennino devoted chapters 10 through 27 to drawing on paper and vellum.

Perhaps the best known of the surviving drawings of the fourteenth century is the *Presentation of the Virgin* in the Louvre (Fig. 7), long considered to have been made by Taddeo Gaddi for his fresco of this subject in S. Croce (Fig. 8).[37] In the course of his study, Oertel attributed the drawing to the so-called Rinuccini Master, who would have copied Taddeo's fresco and then used his drawing as a model for the similar representation of the same subject

7. Taddeo Gaddi (?), *Presentation of the Virgin*. Paris, Louvre.

8. Taddeo Gaddi, *Presentation of the Virgin.* Florence, S. Croce.

that he painted in the Rinuccini Chapel in S. Croce.[38] Even if this new attribution is correct, however, the drawing provides us with a kind of preparatory design that, in view of the number of repeated compositions in Trecento painting, would have constituted an important category. Indeed there has just come to our attention another painting dependent on Taddeo's composition, in addition to the fresco in the Rinuccini Chapel and the miniature by the Limburgs in the *Très Riches Heures*. It is a rather large fresco, made by a local painter, and recently detached from a wall in S. Domenico, Pistoia (Fig. 75, p. 190). It is especially relevant to our discussion because its sinopia was disclosed by detachment of the fresco (Fig. 76, p. 191). This sinopia is very summary, with regard to the buildings as well as the figures, so that the painter could not have arrived at a finished painting containing so many of the forms of the Baroncelli fresco without reference to a drawing much more detailed than the sinopia.

In our opinion the Rinuccini Master, who was the feeblest painter to receive a large commission in Florence in the fourteenth century, could not possibly have executed the strong drawing in the Louvre. Neither he, furthermore, nor any other painter of the third quarter of the century could have captured, or would even have tried to capture, those qualities of Taddeo Gaddi that, despite serious damage, are still apparent in the drawing: the heavy yet buoyant mass of the figures slipping through a deep but loosely structured space. Whether, however, the drawing is by Taddeo himself or by a copyist of his time is exceedingly difficult to ascertain because of its present unsatisfactory condition. The original lines have been overlaid by a web of white, and our hope of establishing more precisely what survives of the original by infra-red photography has been disappointed by the decision of the Louvre not to make such photographs because of the fear of damage to the drawing. Subsequent "restoration" of the drawing is much more extensive than has generally been recognized. In the group of two men standing at the right the torso of the one deeper in space has been drawn over the nearer figure and has been given his right arm, as Oertel has observed. No less crude, however, is the delineation of the folds of the foremost woman kneeling in front of these two men; and the lines on the three children as well as the woman behind them are not by any "maestro dell'arte" of the fourteenth century. Her diaphanous hand is entirely a fabrication of the restorer. On the other hand forms that have not been redrawn, such as the second girl from the right in the portico, are now scarcely visible.

The proportions of the drawing are somewhat more vertical than those of the fresco, which is almost square, but the difference is less than has been claimed because the drawing has been reduced at left and at right and because it contains a strip at the bottom that has no counterpart within the field of the fresco.[39] It has also been said that the drawing could not be a "study" for the fresco because the posture of the Virgin is very different, but in the fresco most of her body has of course been painted by a restorer working on a new patch of intonaco. The fresco in S. Domenico, Pistoia, mentioned above (Fig. 75, p. 190) shows the Virgin as in the Louvre drawing, and proves that the Baroncelli fresco conformed in this respect also.

The child who puts one foot on the first step of the temple extends his arm, in the fresco, in a strange movement. In the drawing this forearm is raised, but even in the reproduction the traces of a lowered arm, as in the fresco, are visible. Furthermore, the raised arm in the drawing appears to be mostly the work of a restorer,[40] but underneath there are lines that indicate that this alternative for the arm existed earlier. Which one was preferred originally cannot now be determined. The existence of these alternatives is especially interesting because this very forearm in the fresco was painted on a separate patch of intonaco (Fig. 74, p. 189). This patch, furthermore, is bounded below by the lower outline of the arm but above approximately by the top of the riser behind. The size of the patch above the arm seems to show that originally part of the arm was higher.[41] The least we can conclude about this patch is that its small size is contrary to normal practice, and it indicates special attention to this detail. Most probably the intonaco was cut out after completion of the figure and a different gesture was painted on a fresh patch. All these facts seem to show that the drawing existed when the fresco was painted.

9. Follower of the Cioni, *Martyrdom of S. Miniato*. New York, Pierpont Morgan Li[brary]

The *Presentation* would not be unique as a drawing of a composition that was afterward painted in fresco. The scene of the martyrdom of S. Miniato by a follower of the Cioni is disposed within a lunette in a drawing in the Morgan Library, New York (Fig. 9). Like the *Presentation* in the Louvre, it is on paper and its forms are fully developed. At present measuring 15⅝ inches wide but cut down to a little more than half its original width, it is large to have been simply a convenient copy of a fresco preserved in a workshop for future use. The subject, furthermore, was so rarely represented — only one other example has survived[42] — that no painter would have bothered to lay by an *exemplum*. The drawing seems remarkably detailed and refined to have served only as a stage preliminary to a fresco, but it must be admitted that we do not know what Trecento conventions with respect to such drawings actually were. Perhaps the *Martyrdom*, as well as the *Presentation*, were *modelli*

26

of the kind mentioned in documents of commission — drawings of a
proposed fresco, presented to a donor and serving as a record of
what the master intended to paint.[43] In 1411 Niccolò di Pietro
Gerini and his associates were required to submit drawings of scenes
they proposed to paint before beginning to work on the wall.[44]

Among the few surviving drawings made before the end of the
Trecento there is a third similar in nature to the *Presentation* and
the *Martyrdom.* It is a drawing of the *Crucifixion* in bistre heightened with white on a brown ground (Fig. 10). Preserved in the
Kupferstichkabinett in Berlin, it is generally attributed to Giovanni

da Milano[45] who, like the authors of the related drawings, was mostly active in Florence. There is, however, no evidence that this drawing was connected with a fresco rather than a panel.

Four scenes from the life of Christ drawn on both sides of two sheets of paper preserved in the British Museum and in the library of Chatsworth have a different character (Fig. 11).[46] Late works of Lippo Vanni, they are drawn in pen and ink, and simply define the figures and the main masses of the landscapes and buildings. They appear to be rapid notations which do not attempt to refine the forms or describe the details. Still more indicative of their original function are the changes in the right-hand part of the *Healing of the Man Born Blind*. After the painter had drawn the water spout and the trough he decided to show the blind man a second time, so that he had to shift the spout farther to the right. Such a change would scarcely occur if the drawing were a copy of an existing representation; it is much more proper to a study for a new work.[47]

11. Lippo Vanni, *Healing of the Man Born Blind*. London, British Museum.

And this work was almost certainly a series of frescoes rather than an altarpiece because the subjects imply an extensive cycle. In the later fourteenth century only one altarpiece (Duomo, Pienza) follows Duccio's *Maestà* by including many scenes of the life of Christ.

These four drawings, in which other small changes occur, are all the more significant because they seem to be the only surviving specimens of the draftsmanship of major Sienese painters. Of the extant corpus of Sienese drawings, 100 percent are apparently studies for frescoes. A similar drawing, though now reduced to the main group of figures, by Spinello Aretino in the Morgan Library, New York, is clearly a "study" for his fresco of 1407–1408 in the Palazzo Pubblico, Siena.[48]

Perhaps, then, practice was more variable than it has seemed. Though much of the preparatory drawing for Trecento frescoes was certainly done on the wall, all of it, we believe, was not. Some projects, especially very large ones of the kind that will be mentioned shortly, were first shaped in small scale. In the instance of less extensive areas, practice probably varied from painter to painter. Vasari himself was of the opinion that "i nostri maestri vecchi . . . avendo spartita tutta l'opera sopra l'arricciato, la disegnavano col pennello, ritraendo da un disegno piccolo tutto quello che volevano fare, con ringrandire a proporzione quanto avevano pensato di mettere in opera . . ." "Having laid out the composition on the *arriccio* they drew it with a brush, taking from a little drawing what they wanted to execute, and enlarging in proportion what they thought to put in the work." The "maestri vecchi" to whom Vasari ascribed this procedure were Simone Martini and other painters of his time.[49]

Closer to the era that concerns us Alberti describes a similar procedure, though as usual he is less close to the technique itself and therefore less explicit.

Et quando aremo a dipigniere storia, prima fra noi molto penseremo, qual modo et quale ordine in quella sia bellissima; et faremo nostri concepti et modelli di tutta la storia et di ciascuna sua parte prima; et chiameremo tutti li amici a consigliarci sopra adciò. Et cosi ci sforz-

12.
Francesco Train
Thebaid (detail)
Pisa, Camposant
Sinopia.

eremo avere ogni parte in noi prima ben pensata, tale che nella opera abbi a essere cosa alchuna, quale non intendiamo ove et come debba essere fatta et conlocata. Et per meglio di tutto avere certezza seguieremo i modelli nostri con paralleli, onde nel publico lavoro torremo da i nostri congetti quasi come da privati commentarij ogni stantia et sito delle cose.

When we have to paint a "storia" we will first think much about what manner and order would make it most beautiful; and we will first make our sketches (*concepti*) and drawings (*modelli*) of the entire "storia" and of each of its parts; and we will call all our friends to advise us about it. And then we will force ourselves to have every part well thought out in our mind from the beginning, so that in the work we will know how each thing ought to be done and where located. In order to have the greater certainty we will inscribe our drawings (*modelli*) with parallels.[50]

Alberti wrote later than Cennino Cennini, and he of course was thinking of the new art while Cennino was talking about the old. Cennino, furthermore, says nothing about drawing prior to that on the *arriccio*, but such drawings were clearly an important stage in the production of mural paintings in the early fifteenth century.

The great usefulness of small compositional drawings is indicated also by the case of the large frescoes, many times the height of a man, a size not unusual in the Trecento. Is it really possible that the first image Giotto shaped of the *Last Judgment* in the Arena Chapel was on the wall itself? Would he have climbed about like a monkey over this large area working up his intricate composition, without a guide to at least the main elements and their scale? Would Traini in the *Thebaid* (Fig. 12) and Nardo in the *Gloria* have followed a similar procedure? The numerous changes in the sinopias of Traini's great Camposanto frescoes, sometimes involving replas-

rancesco Traini,
Thebaid (detail).
sa, Camposanto.
nopia.

tering,[51] concern a figure or a small group of figures (Fig. 13), and they may indicate therefore a lack of drawings of details but not of the whole. The sinopia was the second or third stage of the process of designing, following upon charcoal and often ocher. Still, changes in the sinopia (Fig. 13), or even between a sinopia and the corresponding fresco,[52] are not infrequent. Change is inherent in creativity at all stages, and the presence of it in the sinopia cannot be attributed, as has been done recently, to the lack of previous drawings.[53] More significant is the absence, in sinopias we know, of broad changes, of the transfer of large forms from one part of the composition to another. Aren't these huge frescoes works that demanded layout before the approach to the wall?

The need for small drawings of at least the large forms in a composition would seem urgent also when frescoes were not prepared by sinopia drawings. The progress of the campaign of conservation in Tuscany has already shown that such cases, contrary to Cennini, were not rare. No sinopia was found, for instance, below the frescoes of the *Way to Calvary*, the *Suicide of Judas*, or the *Flagellation* in the style of Nardo in the Badia in Florence. A sinopia was not used for the large *Last Judgment* over the last altar on the left nave wall in S. Domenico, Pistoia. This fresco, painted by a Pistoiese master influenced by Cristiani, shows no traces of a *spolvero*, no incisions (except on the haloes), and very little drawing on the intonaco.

Historians who deny the existence of small compositional drawings must explain also how a certain kind of building in perspective was laid out on the wall. In Giotto's paintings in the Peruzzi Chapel, as in some later Trecento frescoes, groups of architectural orthogonals converge in small areas beyond the paintings themselves. In the *Birth and Naming of St. John* the distance of these areas from the nearer frame equals a half or three quarters of the width of the fresco. The fresco, of course, is as wide as the wall of the chapel, so that the areas of convergence are in outer space, so to speak, either in the transept of the church or in the garden behind it. Even if there were sinopia drawings — actually they are lacking — the problem is evident.

14. Pietro di Puccio, *Coronation of the Virgin* (detail). Pisa, Camposanto. Sinopia.

Replicas of pictorial compositions, sometimes nearly identical with the original, were not uncommon in the fourteenth century. When the model was a fresco and hence immovable, and the copy had to be executed at a distance, an intermediate drawing was required, as in the case of the *Presentation of the Virgin* in Pistoia (Fig. 75, p. 190). Several drawings made at the end of the century as copies of frescoes in S. Francesco, Assisi,[54] must have served this purpose, or the closely related one of providing the painter with a model that could be used as the point of departure for a more or less similar composition. It has indeed been shown that the practice of making portable copies — presumably drawings — of mural paintings was established early in the fourteenth century.[55] Figures in frescoes were repeated in panels painted some distance away, and repetition must have occurred in frescoes also. Drawings of this kind must have played a not unimportant part, prior to the sinopia, in the preparation of fresco paintings.

Does not all this prove that although Trecento painters were undeniably accustomed to lay out their compositions on the wall, they did not always begin there but occasionally at least, for one purpose or another, they utilized drawings in small scale on paper or some other material? The sinopias constitute the great glory of late medieval Italian draftsmanship, but admiration and the excitement at their discovery should not lead us to ignore the evidence for the use of less monumental but still significant forms of preparatory drawings.

NOTES

1. For a good review of our knowledge of ancient mural techniques see M. H. Swindler, *Ancient Painting*, New Haven, 1929, pp. 417–427.

2. Vitruvius, VII, 3; see *Vitruvius on Architecture* (Loeb Library), London, 1934, II, p. 93.

3. In the course of his discussion of the preparation of walls for plastering, Vitruvius (*op. cit.*, p. 97), describes a technique similar to one occasionally used in the Trecento. The movement of timber partitions, he says, produces cracks in plaster,

and these can be prevented by the use underneath of two layers of reeds fixed crosswise and held by broadheaded nails. The terrible fire during the war in the Camposanto in Pisa disclosed a similar application of reeds, in this case between the plaster and the wall (Fig. 13). The purpose of the reeds in the Camposanto was to insulate the plaster from the moisture of the wall, which is exposed to the weather on its outer side.

4. Pliny, xxxv, 18; cf. *Pliny, Natural History* (Loeb Library), London, 1952, IX, p. 273.

5. XXXV, 48; *op. cit.*, p. 297.

6. Among recently published opinions see L. V. Borrelli, "Un nuovo frammento dei paesaggi dell' Odissea," *Bollettino d'Arte*, XLI, 1956, p. 299; P. W. Lehmann, *Roman Wall Paintings from Boscoreale in the Metropolitan Museum of Art*, Cambridge (Mass.), 1953, p. 164; W. Klinkert, "Bemerkungen zur Technik der Pompejanischen Wanddekoration," in L. Curtius, *Die Wandmalerei Pompejis*, Hildesheim, 1960, pp. 435–472; S. Augusti, "La tecnica dell' antica pittura parietale pompeiana," in *Pompeiana, Raccolta di studi per il secondo centenario degli scavi di Pompei*, Naples, 1950, pp. 313–354. I am indebted for these references to Professors Homer Thompson and Peter von Blanckenhagen. Klinkert inclines to believe that Vitruvius's discussion of painting on wet plaster refers only to the monochromatic large rectangular fields. A. P. Laurie, *The Technique of the Great Painters*, London, 1959, p. 35 ff., maintains, however, that much of Roman painting was executed in the *buon fresco* described by Vitruvius.

7. These possibilities, already emphasized by A. P. Laurie (*Greek and Roman Methods of Painting*, Cambridge, 1910, p. 94), have not been sufficiently taken into account in the recent studies by S. Augusti, in *Napoli, Palazzo Reale*, IV *Mostra di Restauri*, Naples, 1960, p. 27.

8. The label "frescoes" that Swindler, *op. cit.*, figs. 532–535, cautiously applies to these paintings needs no quotation marks. A. Maiuri, *La villa dei misteri*, Rome, 1931, pp. 206–208, claimed that the paintings were executed in *buon fresco*. On the other hand R. Herbig, *Neue Beobachtungen am Fries der Mysterien-Villa in Pompeji*, Baden-Baden, 1958, p. 15 ff., pointed to the fact that in several places small pieces of the colors of the figures, their garments, or the objects they hold have peeled, exposing in each case a color similar to that of the adjacent background. He concluded that the architectural background was painted in one campaign, the figures years later in another, executed *a secco* over the preexisting background. The phenomena that Herbig observed – not in the part of the frieze reproduced here (Fig. 1, pp. 4–5) – may, we believe, be interpreted in another way; we hope to discuss the question on another occasion.

9. See E. Berger, *Quellen und Technik der Fresko-, Oel-, und Tempera-Malerei des Mittelalters*, 2nd edition, Munich, 1912, p. 90. Mr. Andrew Petryn kindly informs us that the paintings from Doura in the Yale University Collection were executed *a secco*, without a strong binding material. No

intonaco was employed in these.

Laurie, *op. cit.*, p. 41, points to the important possibility that rewetting a largely dry intonaco may float some particles of lime from below the surface to it, where they then undergo carbonation. If this process occurs extensively it may help to account for the durability of much medieval fresco secco.

10. Theophilus, chap. xv: ". . . Cum imagines vel aliarum rerum effigies pertrahuntur in muro sicco, statim aspergatur aqua, tam diu donec omnino madidus sit. Et in eodem humore liniantur omnes colores, qui supponendi sunt, qui omnes calce misceantur, et cum ipso muro siccentur ut haereant . . ." Cf. Theophilus Presbyter, *Schedula diversarum artium*, ed. by A. Ilg, Vienna, 1874, p. 33. See also Berger, *op. cit.*, p. 51, and R. Oertel, "Wandmalerei und Zeichnung in Italien," *Mitteilungen des Kunsthistorischen Instituts in Florenz*, v. 1940, p. 277. For the dating of this text in the eleventh century see B. Bischoff, "Die Uberlieferung des Theophilus-Rugerus nach den ältesten Handschriften," *Münchner Jahrbuch der bildenden Kunst*, III–IV, 1952–1953, pp. 145–149.

11. Oertel, *op. cit.*, p. 276 ff.

12. Bands of intonaco as large as many square meters have been observed in the paintings in the Kariye Camii (R. J. Gettens and G. L. Stout, "A Monument of Byzantine Wall Painting – the Method of Construction," *Studies in Conservation*, III, 1958, p. 118). Smaller rectangles may be seen in the paintings in the Cappella di S. Silvestro, SS. Quattro Coronati, Rome.

Oertel's estimate of medieval techniques is based upon the belief that the *pontata* requires a rapid preliminary drawing, presumably because the intonaco dries in a relatively short time (*op. cit.*, p. 280), but a *pontata* is entirely compatible with secco drawing as well as painting.

13. See E. Borsook, *The Mural Painters of Tuscany*, London, 1960, p. 128; also p. 14.

14. Only one coat instead of the usual two or more, according to Borsook, *loc. cit.* See above note 3, on the use of reeds in ancient Rome and in the Italian Trecento (Pisa) to prevent such damage.

15. Observed by Borsook, *op. cit.*, p. 128.

16. In the *Sacrifice of Abraham* a suture may be discerned at the level of the waist of Abraham, and then it descends along the right side of Isaac, following the outline of the figure.

17. Oertel, *op. cit.*, p. 281.

18. Gettens and Stout, *op. cit.*, pp. 114, 118. See also the Cionesque *Resurrection* formerly in S. M. Novella, discussed by Borsook, *op. cit.*, p. 21.

19. Unfortunately the scaffold barely brought us to the level of this fresco and did not make possible a study of its center or left section.

20. U. Procacci, *La tecnica degli antichi affreschi e il loro distacco e restauro*, Florence, 1958, p. 10, pl. XI. Traces of the use of *spolvero* in a panel by Domenico are visible in the *Madonna* in the National Gallery, Washington (Fig. 6). The telltale dots of color may be seen in the upper lids of the eyes of the Child and along the upper lip.

21. *Ibid.* It should be pointed out, furthermore, that in chapter 141 of

his treatise Cennino Cennini describes the technique of *spolvero* for the design of drapery on panels. Vellum punctured by a needle serves as the stencil. One of the examples of Orcagnesque *spolveri* is reproduced by Borsook, *op. cit.*, pl. III(c).

22. Quoted from the translation by D. V. Thompson, Jr., *Il libro dell' arte*, New Haven, II, 1933, pp. 42–44. For the Italian text see *idem*, I, 1932, pp. 40–42.

23. *Le Vite*, ed. Milanesi, Florence, 1906, I, pp. 181–182.

24. "Questo (affresco) all' aria si purga, e dall' acqua si difende, e regge di continuo a ogni percossa." *Ibid.*

25. "Vuole ancora una mano destra, risoluta e veloce, ma sopra tutto un giudizio saldo e intiero. . . ." *Loc. cit.*

26. *Op. cit.*, I, p. 558. This work by Simone ". . . si rimase imperfetto e disegnato, come insino a oggi si può vedere, di rossaccio col pennello in su l'arricciato . . . così molte altre ne sono che erano state dipinte, le quali, scrostatosi poi il lavoro, sono rimase così disegnate di rossaccio sopra l'arricciato."

27. The influence of preparatory drawing in mosaic technique upon sinopia was pointed out by Berger, *op. cit.*, pp. 91, 113, and later by Oertel, *op. cit.*, p. 273.

28. See Borsook, *op. cit.*, p. 20. The angel at the center of the *Last Judgment* and two coffins in the *Triumph of Death* were redrawn on a thin layer of fresh intonaco.

29. *Op. cit.*, I, p. 558.

30. Borsook, *op. cit.*, p. 144.

31. *Op. cit.*, p. 75.

32. For instance, Berenson, *Draw-ings of the Florentine Painters*, Chicago, 1938, II, p. 79, no. 758.

33. Oertel, *op. cit.*, p. 272 ff. He does point out (p. 231 ff.) that the repetition of certain Franciscan scenes implies a dependence on drawings because there were no miniatures of these subjects. He also cites (p. 244 ff.) drawings of the end of the century that served to transmit part or all of a composition, or were used in connection with a contract.

34. For reproductions of these works see Van Marle, *Development of the Italian Schools*, III, figs. 190, 191 (frescoes, S. Croce); *De Giotto à Bellini* (Orangerie des Tuileries), Paris, 1956, fig. 9 (*Nativity*, Dijon); *Catalogo della Mostra Giottesca* (1937), Florence, (1943), fig. 141a (*Annunciation*, Pistoia).

35. R. Offner, *Corpus of Florentine Painting*, New York, Section III, vol. III, 1930, pl. XIV.[25]

36. A. Blum, *On the origin of paper*, New York, 1934, pp. 32–36; F. Hoyer, *Einführung in die Papierkunde*, Leipzig, 1914, pp. 20–28; R. H. Clapperton, *Paper: An Historical Account of Its Making by Hand from the Earliest Times down to the Present Day*, Oxford, 1934, pp. 74–82. For the conversion around 1370 of *lire bolognesi* into Florentine florins (the rate was 5/13) see C. M. Cipolla, *Studi di storia della moneta: I movimenti dei cambi in Italia dal secolo XIII al XV*, Pavia, 1948, pp. 51–52. In 1385 Spinello Aretino received 100 fiorini for an altarpiece (Vasari, *Vite*, ed. Milanesi, I, p. 689 note). In 1367–1368 it was agreed that 40 florins were to be paid to Orcagna for a triptych for Or S. Michele, and the sum of over 200 lire was paid for

the *Coronation of the Virgin* for the Mint, now in the Accademia (O. Sirèn, *Giottino*, Leipzig, 1908, pp. 101–102). For the payments received by Sienese painters around 1375 see for instance G. Milanesi, *Documenti per la storia dell' arte senese*, Siena, 1854, I, pp. 269, 292.

37. Berenson, *loc. cit.*; *Commemorative Catalogue of the Exhibition of Italian Art* (drawings ed. by A. E. Popham), London, 1930, I, p. 200. The view that the drawing preceded the fresco has been maintained by R. Bacou and J. Bean, *Dessins florentins de la collection de Filippo Baldinucci*, Paris, 1958, p. 15 and *idem*, *Disegni fiorentini del museo del Louvre*, Rome, 1959, p. 32. The attribution to Taddeo has been maintained by Meiss, *Painting in Florence and Siena after the Black Death*, Princeton, 1951, p. 28 n. 56.

38. *Op. cit.*, p. 236. Charles de Tolnay (*History and Technique of Old Master Drawings*, New York, 1943, p. 106) agrees with Oertel's opinion that the drawing is a copy from the fresco, but he rejects the attribution to the Rinuccini Master.

39. Oertel interpreted the more vertical proportions of the drawing and the award of a halo to the High Priest as changes consistent with the style of the Rinuccini Master. It is true that the halo, if attributable to the original draftsman rather than the restorer, diminishes the recession of the temple, but neither of these departures from Taddeo's fresco are, however, apparent in the fresco in the Rinuccini Chapel. On the other hand the most striking change in the Rinuccini fresco, the revolution of the figure of the Vir-

gin so that instead of facing towards her parents (as she does in S. Croce) she faces the High Priest, is not made in the drawing. This eagerness of the Virgin to mount the steps to the Priest is characteristic of the representations of the third quarter of the century (Meiss, *op. cit.*, pp. 27–29).

40. In the drawing the figure of the youth in the lower-left corner has a raised right hand rather than a left, as in the fresco. It is difficult to be certain whether this is the consequence of a misunderstanding by the restorer (as seems probable), or whether it reflects original alternatives.

41. We are much indebted for this observation to Mr. Robert Janson-La Palme, who has mapped the *giornate* in the Baroncelli Chapel in the course of his preparation of a study of it.

42. Altarpiece by Jacopo del Casentino, S. Miniato, Florence. In both instances hot oil is ladled in the saint's ear. G. Kaftal, *Iconography of the Saints in Tuscan Painting*, Florence, 1952, p. 747 (the drawing is not cited here) erroneously says that in the scene in the altarpiece nails are driven into the saint's eardrums.

43. As proposed by Meiss, in *One Hundred Master Drawings*, ed. by A. Mongan, Cambridge (Mass.), 1949, p. 2. Berenson (*op. cit.*, II, p. 353, no. 2756C) earlier described the drawing as a model for a fresco, but erroneously attributed it to Spinello Aretino.

44. R. Piattoli, "Un mercante del Trecento e gli artisti del tempo suo," *Rivista d'Arte*, XII, 1930, p. 126.

45. The drawing measures 285 x 222 mm. See O. Sirèn, "Florentiner Trecentozeichnungen," *Jahrbuch der Preussischen Kunstsammlungen*, XXVII, 1906, p. 208 ff.; Berenson, *op. cit.*, II, p. 96 no. 905B; A. Marabottini, *Giovanni da Milano*, Florence, 1950, p. 82, pl. xv.

46. Meiss, "Nuovi dipinti e vecchi problemi," *Rivista d'arte*, XXX, 1955, pp. 137–142; P. Pouncey, in *Burlington Magazine*, LXXXVIII, 1946, pp. 168–172.

47. This view was expressed by Pouncey, *loc. cit.*, and Meiss, *loc. cit.*

48. Oertel, *op. cit.*, p. 248, fig. 11. No exception to the statement made above about Sienese drawings need be made for the drawing in the British museum attributed tentatively to Siena by A. E. Popham and P. Pouncey, *Italian Drawings in the British Museum*, London, 1950, no. 267, pl. 229. It seems rather to be a rare specimen of Riminese, or at least Romano-Florentine, draftsmanship.

49. *Op. cit.*, I, p. 558.

50. L. B. Alberti's *Kleinere Kunsttheoretische Schriften*, ed. by H. Janitschek, Vienna, 1877, p. 159. The above translation is based, especially with regard to the difficult last sentence, on that by J. R. Spencer, *L. B. Alberti On Painting*, New Haven, 1956, p. 96.

Borsook (*op. cit.*, p. 26) relates to this passage another in which Alberti says that small drawings conceal large weaknesses while large drawings expose small weaknesses (Alberti, ed. *cit.*, p. 153). Dr. Borsook deduces from this statement that Alberti would have approved of large-scale sinopias and also that

he would have advised painters not to enlarge their compositions from plans prepared on a smaller scale. It should, however, be pointed out that the statment about drawing on small and large scale appears in a different context, at another point in his text. After recommending drawing from nature Alberti speaks of learning to draw, and urges the painter to practice by drawing things large, not on "tavolelle," for the reason set forth in the sentence paraphrased at the beginning of this note. Learning to draw, by "taking from nature," is a different aspect of artistry than planning mural compositions, a task which presents its own distinctive set of problems, and we are not convinced that what Alberti says about one process is relevant to what he says about the other (as summarized in the text above).

51. See note 28.

52. See the sinopia and the fresco in the lunette of the Porta di S. Giorgio, Florence (Procacci, *op. cit.*, pls. IV–V). In Masolino's sinopia for the *Decapitation of St. Catherine* in S. Clemente, Rome, the saint is prone, whereas in the fresco itself she kneels. Two figures appearing at the sides of the tree in Duccio's drawing of the *Entry into Jerusalem* (disclosed by infra-red photography) were not introduced into the painting. The width of the road was greatly altered also (see *Il restauro della "Maestà" di Duccio*, Rome, 1959, pl. xxxI).

53. See the discussion by Oertel (*op. cit.*, p. 290) of the *Coronation* by Pietro di Puccio in the Camposanto, Pisa (Fig. 14).

54. B. Degenhart, "Autonome Zeich-

nungen bei mittelalterlichen Künstlern," *Münchner Jahrbuch der bildenden Kunst*, 1, 1950, p. 98; Tolnay, *op. cit.*, p. 105, no. 16.

55. Meiss, *Giotto and Assisi*, New York, 1960, p. 3 f., and "Reflections of Assisi: A Tabernacle and the Cesi Master," in *Scritti d'arte in onore di Mario Salmi* (in the press).

CHAPTER 2

The Cycle as a Whole

ALMOST a hundred years ago Cavalcaselle, summarizing his judgment of the scenes of the *Legend* in the Upper Church, said: ". . . as the life of St. Francis unfolds itself, the power of the artists increases . . . until, towards the close, an art apparently new . . . reveals the development of the talent of Giotto."[1] Few recent historians follow the great Italian critic's estimate of the gradual emergence of Giotto in the course of the cycle but all are agreed that the twenty-eight scenes show some kind of an evolution. For the majority of scholars the direction of change is from Scene II to Scene XXVIII. In other words, with the exception of Scene I, recognized as anomalous already by Cavalcaselle, the chronology of the painting of the frescoes is believed to have coincided with the chronology of the successive episodes in the life of the saint.

So powerful is the impetus of the narrative, and so salient the nature of the changes in it, that an execution progressing around the walls of the nave, moving eastward on the north wall, across the east or façade wall, and then westward on the south wall, has usually been assumed without comment. Such a procedure differed however from the one employed for the tier of frescoes above the *Legend*. Though absolute proof is lacking, no one doubts that the Old Testament scenes on the north wall and the New Testament scenes on the south wall were produced in the same sequence if not in exact chronological correspondence; the painters worked on both walls from the transept to the façade. Of course the scenes on these opposite walls do not compose a compact narrative sequence. But in at least one great medieval monument where the narrative, like the *Legend*, does wind continuously around the nave and entrance walls, the order of execution does not conform with the order of the narrative. If the conclusions of Otto Demus about the Old Testament mosaics in the Cathedral of Monreale are correct, work proceeded on the south wall from east to west, in conformity with the narrative, but on the north wall work proceeded in the same direction, and thus contrary to the story.[2]

If, then, work on the *Legend* moved from Scenes II to XXVIII, the procedure was not conventional but represented an unusual if not unprecedented practice. Not all historians, however, have read the sequence in this way; just recently, in fact, a schedule involving parallel execution from west to east, as in the frescoes of the upper tier, has been proposed again.[3] The judgment of the direction of the work is, of course, bound up with conceptions of authorship. For all these reasons, then, proof of the sequence of the work would advance the criticism of the frescoes.

The order of execution of the three or four frescoes in a bay is readily determined by the structure of adjacent patches. In our reproductions of successive scenes patches common to both are, of course, given the same number. The smaller part of the patch is distinguished as PREC. if the larger part is in the preceding scene, and FOLL. if the larger part is in the following scene. Thus in Scene II patches 2 FOLL. and 3 FOLL., most of which are in Scene III, overlap 2, 5, and 10 in Scene II (Figs. 29, p. 87, 30, p. 89). It is therefore certain that Scene III was painted after Scene II. In Scene V (Fig. 32, p. 93) 3, 5, 8, 9, and 10 overlap 2 PREC. and 4 PREC., most of which are in Scene IV. Scene V was thus painted after Scene IV. The lower part of the column between VII and VIII was prepared after VII and before VIII. In some cases the intonaco for much of the column between two scenes was laid before the adjacent parts of the scenes. Thus the column between XXVI and XXVII was prepared in fresco before 2, 5, and 7 in XXVI (Fig. 53, p. 151), and before 2, 3, 4, and 5 in XXVII (Fig. 54, p. 153). However, in XXVI, 1 FOLL., which contains the capital of this column as well as a small part of the background of XXVI, though it extends far into XXVII, overlaps 1 in XXVI. XXVI was thus clearly painted before XXVII.

Relationships of this kind are constant – with one exception – within the bays of the cycle, indicating that within these bays the scenes were painted in the order of the narrative. The exceptional fresco is Scene I (Fig. 26, p. 77). Patches 2 FOLL. and 6 FOLL., which extend far into Scene II, lie under 3, 8, 10, and 13 in Scene I (See Diagram B, p. 195). Furthermore the intonaco of the corbel table below Scene I was laid after that of Scene II. The painting of the corbel table confirms the separateness of Scene I. The forms were intended to match those in the moldings below Scenes II and III, but the colors – the grays and blues – diverge noticeably. We shall return later to other aspects of Scene I.

While the establishment of the sequence of frescoes within each of the bays presented no problem, determination of the sequence between bays proved more difficult. The bays are divided by a bundle of five engaged columns (Fig. 15). The stone columns were covered with plaster and painted. The sutures in the crevices between columns, or between the columns and the wall, are much less easy to read because of the comparative roughness and carelessness of the plastering and the painting. But all the discoverable evidence points to the same sequence between bays as within the bays. This sequence was maintained in the relation between nave walls and façade; in other words, Scene XIV on the entrance wall was painted after the adjacent XIII on the north wall, and XV on the entrance wall was painted before the adjacent XVI on the south wall (see Diagram A).

One link in the chain has not, for practical reasons, been controlled. Examination of the medallions and ornamental frescoes over the entrance doors between XIV and XV would have required a higher scaffold than we possessed and would have interfered with passage in and out of the church. Such an examination did not appear to be required for many reasons, some of which will appear later in the course of the discussion. Inasmuch as the work proceeded from II to XIV and from XV to XXVIII the only alternative to a sequence in which XV followed XIV would be a simultaneous beginning at II and at XV (see Diagram A). This is a priori improbable, and indeed on grounds of style impossible. The exceptionally weak assistant who

15. *The Life of St. Francis*, Scenes IV–VI.
Assisi, S. Francesco.

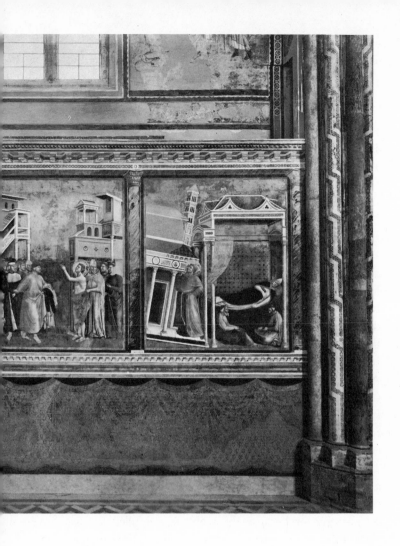

is conspicuous in 15 in Scene XIII (Fig. 40*b*, p. 117) but not in the first scenes on this wall appears again in 11 of XVI across the church (Fig. 42, p. 121). This fact proves continuity from XIII to XVI.

Topographical evidence thus confirms the stylistic judgments of the majority of scholars about sequence in the cycle of St. Francis. Even the usual view of Scene I, which is associated with Scenes XXVI–XXVIII, is at least partly confirmed; it is, we have shown, later than Scene II, and we shall shortly prove its connection with the opposite wall. Our findings have thus not at this point contributed new ideas, but the proof, not commonly obtainable, of judgments based on style seems significant as validation of the art historian's methods.

The scenes in the cycle, exhibiting considerable stylistic change at certain points as the work progressed, are nevertheless contained in a remarkably unified framework. This framework extends over the entire wall from the floor to the catwalk above. Simulated drapery, hanging from the corbel table, covers the lowest part of the wall (Fig. 16). It is painted chiefly in fresco, each patch corresponding in width more or less to the scene above (see Diagram A). The corbel table and the entablature are painted largely in fresco, but the columns between the scenes were only prepared in fresco. They were completed *a secco*, with pigments that included, for the light parts, white lead, which has as usual darkened. The seventh bay (Scenes XXIII–XXV) is, however, exceptional (Figs. 49, p. 141, 51, p. 145, 52, p. 149). The four columns in this bay, except for a small part of the first column, preserve the high values that all the columns originally possessed, either because they were painted in *buon fresco* or because the white lead applied *a secco* has been rubbed down by a restorer, exposing unoxydized pigment below it.

These spiral columns at first seem all alike in design, but in actuality they fall into two categories, distinguished by what we might call the height of their wave-length in profile. Those with shallower indentations and projections may be called "rigid," the others "sinuous." These two types are distributed in identical fashion on both walls; in other words, opposite bays correspond exactly (see Diagram A).

A similar adherence to an overall plan is manifested by other de-

16. *The Life of St. Francis*, detail of simulated corbel table and drapery. Assisi, S. Francesco.

tails as well as by the more obvious architectural forms. Just above the painted cornice a molding containing a series of four-pointed stars extends over the twenty-eight frescoes. This molding is carved stone over the first two bays, that is, over Scenes I–VI, and it is painted to simulate stone over Scenes VII–XIII (see Diagram A). A corresponding sequence obtains on the opposite wall: carved over Scenes XXVII–XXIII, painted over Scenes XXII–XVI.

It is quite possible that the stone molding existed in the first two bays (A and B) before the painters arrived on the scene. But a similar symmetry in the two walls has been observed in the columns, and it extends to other painted forms as well. The capitals in the first three bays (A, B, C) are all alike. In the last bay on both walls (D), however, a variation is introduced (see Diagram A). Each of these two bays has five columns instead of four. Only the center capital is like those in the other bays; the two at each side are reduced in size and complexity, so as to emphasize the center capital (Figs. 17, 18). These smaller capitals are employed also in the two scenes on the entrance wall between these bays, XIV and XV.

The symmetry of the shapes of the capitals is maintained in the principles of lighting. The capitals are lighted either from the left or the right (Figs. 17, 18), and in this respect too there is perfect correspondence of the two walls (see Diagram A). Light and shade are in this regard controlled not by reference to the actual source of light but by a desire for symmetry within each bay or between bays.

17. *"Large" capital,* center of Bay D.   18. *"Small" capital,* at left in Bay D.

Thus both capitals in Scene XIV receive light from the left, though a large door exists immediately to the right. A similar relationship may be observed in Scene XV, so that the lighting on the entrance wall is symmetrical but not naturalistic.

The *Legend* was painted over a considerable period of time by a succession of at least three masters possessing distinctive styles, not to mention numerous more mediocre painters. One master began at Scene II (if not in the original Scene I), another made a decisive entrance in XX, and a third in XXVI. But we have seen that in the framework at least, one plan governed the whole. Perhaps these enframing and decorative areas were executed by one painter or team of painters who remained throughout the enterprise. Perhaps, on the other hand, various painters in succession executed these surfaces, modeling their work on preceding scenes and guided by a drawn scheme of the whole, adherence to which was enforced by the abbot or someone else in authority. The existence of a recorded scheme for the cycle is suggested also by the correspondence on the two long walls of one aspect of the scenes themselves, as indicated by the diagram. Indeed the only alternative to a diagram or drawing of the cycle would be the continuous presence of one *peintre-en-chef*, who would himself impose uniformity and correspondence. The constant presence of such a painter however would imply either greater continuity of style than is actually visible in the frescoes, or a crash program with many painters working at once on different parts of the cycle. All the evidence seems to show that the frescoes were not produced in this way.

It is clear, however, that the scenes themselves do not conform to the scheme for the framework in one important respect. The incidence of the light is not arranged symmetrically within each bay, as in the instance of the capitals on both long walls. In bays B, C, and D on both walls the chief source of light is from the left or the east. In A on both walls it comes from the west. Thus the dominant movement of light in the scenes often conflicts with the light on the capitals. It might seem that the light in the scenes is more naturalistically conceived, coming from the portals in bays B, C, and D, and from the choir in A. But the source in Scene xiv is at the left, while the portal is at the right. Furthermore the incidence in Scenes xiv and xv is identical, not, as in the capitals alongside these scenes, symmetrical. It should be said, moreover, that the lighting within each of the scenes is not always consistent. We have considered the dominant direction to be that which controls the figures. In one scene indeed, xxvi, which is exceptional, the light on the figures at the left comes from the left and on those at the right from the right. Often the architecture does not conform. In Scene xxiv the source for the figures is at the left, but the bier is lighted from the right. The figures in xxv have the same source as the figures in xxiv, but the building seems lighted from both sides. The same kind of opposition between figures and architecture may be observed in Scene xviii.

The remarkable unity exhibited in the framework of the cycle and extended, as we have seen, to such aspects of the scenes as the source of the light falling on the figures raises the question of the length of time over which the frescoes were painted. Our topographical analysis enables us only to approximate a minimum. It is, in other words, impossible to prove that interruptions of considerable duration did not occur. The total number of *giornate* we have traced within the scenes is 272. No doubt this figure is, as we have said, slightly low, because a few of the hair-line sutures in Scenes xx–xxv have escaped us. Joints are also difficult to discern below paint, such as white, that is laid heavily.

The translation of these 272 patches into actual working time is subject to two qualifications. First, certain kinds of patches probably did not require a day. In Scene v, for instance, patches 1 and 2, containing parts of the entablature, of the green and red borders around the scenes, and of the background, might well have been partly carried out in one day. The plasterer might have spread the intonaco for 1 in the morning, and then, while the painter worked there, he spread the intonaco for 2. The painter, having completed 1, moved over during the course of the day to 2. It is also possible that, after the intonaco for 2 was spread, a second painter came up on the scaffold to go to work on it immediately, but if this were the procedure the reason for a vertical joint between 1 and 2 is not evident. In a few instances, on the other hand, the execution in one day of two small adjacent patches containing very similar forms has seemed to us so probable that we have given them the same number. Good examples are the hands of St. Francis – 6 in Scene XII, and 8 in Scene xv (Figs. 39*b*, p. 114 and 41, p. 119).

Execution of two or more patches on the same day would not necessarily be limited to patches within a fresco but might extend, under certain conditions, to patches in adjacent frescoes. The scaffold probably extended the width of a bay, and simultaneous execution of two frescoes would be possible when the column between them was painted first, or where, as in Scenes xxvi–xxviii by the St. Cecilia Master, the patches of each scene were contained within the rectangles of the borders (Figs. 53–55, pp. 151–155). Such practices are not to be found on the first wall. There, however, it is possible that the reversal of the normal left-to-right sequence to right-to-left in patches 7–12 of Scene XII was motivated by the wish to execute Scene XIII in as close a succession as possible (Diagram E).

If all these possibilities would reduce somewhat our 272 working days, another phase of the painting beyond doubt considerably increased them. Our *giornate* give us a tally only of the painting done *ad affresco*, whereas of course much of the surface, like the blue backgrounds and the columns, was only prepared in fresco but finished *a secco*. Many small forms, furthermore, were painted entirely on the dry wall, as we shall point out in Chapter iv. More than one master could work *a secco* on one scene; the number would be controlled chiefly by convenience on the several levels of the scaffold and the amount of repeated detail, as in drapery hanging flat against a wall, or of invariable color, as in buildings and backgrounds. One of the leading masters would of course reserve for himself the completion *a secco* of the mantles of central figures.

All these considerations do not permit a precise estimate even of the minimum time required for the painting of the cycle. To the days spent on the stages of the work already discussed must be added the time devoted to preparation of the designs, whether first on small scale or in sinopias — no traces of which, as a matter of fact, have yet been detected. In view of all this a year would seem to be about the minimum time imaginable for the twenty-eight frescoes, and that would imply a relentless application. Almost certainly the work took much longer than that.

Though the painted architecture surrounding the twenty-eight scenes is exactly alike in opposite scenes on the two main walls, the scenes themselves do not maintain this correspondence, either in style, as has frequently been observed, or in the mosaic of the intonaco. The most obvious difference between the two walls is the occurrence on the south wall of scenes with many more patches than on the north wall. On the north wall the number ranges from 6 in Scene iv to 14 or 15; only Scene xiii exceeds this limit, with 21 (Diagrams B–E). But on the south wall one scene (xx) has more than double the number of patches used in xiii, while xviii has 29, xxiii has 21, and two others have 19 (Diagrams G–J). The variation, too, on this wall is much greater, for xix has only 8 and xxv 10.

The number of patches is in large measure a function of the number of figures in a scene and the complexity of the setting. This fact becomes clear upon perusal of the diagrams (B–J, pp. 195 ff) where the number of figures, sometimes perforce approximate, is recorded alongside the number of patches. But the matter is more complex than these two sets of quantities indicate. Thus Scene XIII, with 21 patches, has 20 figures, exclusive of small segments of heads, while XX, with 54 patches, has about 47 figures. This would appear to be an almost one-to-one relation in both frescoes. Such an estimate, however, would mask an important difference between the "intonaco style" of the two frescoes, because in XIII 7 of the 21 patches do not contain any of the 20 figures, while every patch in XX has a part of a figure.

Further observations about differences in the "intonaco style" of the chief painters will be made in the following chapter. One large divergence within the cycle should, however, be pointed out here. In Scenes II–XV the lowest patch or patches invariably include at least part of the ground plane (Diagrams B–F). In all but XIII the patch extends down into the corbel table, and sometimes up a short distance above the ground plane. In all the scenes on the south wall, on the other hand, the lowest patches end exactly where the scene does: in other words at the green border that bounds each one (Diagrams G–J).

In this respect Scene I, which we have proved to be exceptional, is unique on the north wall and similar to all the scenes on the south wall (Fig. 28, p. 83). This scene was certainly painted later than Scene II, and probably around the time that the St. Cecilia Master was working on XXVI–XXVIII. The question remains whether the present Scene I replaces an original fresco that was painted at the beginning of the cycle by the master of Scene II and then subsequently cut out, or whether the space was reserved for later execution of the present fresco. The rather straight edges of the patches at the right (3, 8, 10) do not solve the question. Professor Gnudi has made the interesting suggestion that painting of this scene was delayed until the rood beam was set.[4]

The difference between the two walls with regard to the lowest patches is not insignificant artistically. In most of the scenes from II to XV the feet are separated from the body and painted in the same patch as the ground (Diagrams B–F). Termination of the patches at the border of the scene in xvi–xxviii facilitates the unification of feet, legs, and torso (Diagrams G–J). In an art concerned with the realization of weight and support this unification of the figure must be regarded as a significant advance. We are not surprised to see it maintained in the Arena Chapel, the Baroncelli Chapel (which we have been able to examine while this book was in the press), and, later, in Masaccio's *Expulsion of Adam and Eve*.[5] It should be noted that the unification was already accomplished in Scene ii, largely because of the lack of a distinctive ground plane, and that it was not on the other hand accomplished in Scene i, no doubt because of an exceptional activity in the ground plane, which includes much of the poor man and his mantle.

The varying level of the lowest patches is the most consistent, but not the only, difference in the intonaco pattern of the two walls. On the north wall the patches often extend laterally across the borders between scenes; on the south wall they end more often at the vertical borders, as they always do at the lower horizontal one. And of course this termination of the patches at the lower frame has its effect on the levels of the patches above. There tend to be three bands of patches in the scenes on the south wall. These bands probably correspond to three levels of the scaffold. Since the height of the scenes, from green border to green borders, is 3.50 m. or 11½ feet, each band would be almost 4 feet high if they were equal in height. Actually they vary considerably, but not extending to a height of more than 5 feet, so that the surface can be conveniently covered by a man remaining on one platform. The patches on the north wall, on the other hand, extend to a greater total height because they include part at least of the corbel table, and they seem to fall into four bands, implying one more platform than was employed on the opposite wall.

The actual height of the most frequently recurring form in the cycle — the human figure — varies considerably, but bears no constant relation to the major levels of the patches in the scenes. The tallest figures appear in those scenes in which there are the fewest: in Scenes ii and xv, where the figures measure about 65 and 64 inches, respectively (see table, p. 58). The figure measures 65 inches also in Scene v, though here the figures are numerous. It is notable that in Scene xiv, which corresponds on the entrance wall to Scene xv, the figure is considerably shorter. In Scene viii the exceptionally short figures may be attributed to the space required by the fiery chariot over their heads.

The most consistently short figures in the cycle appear in Scenes xx–xxiv. Here the heights vary from about 53 to 58 inches. It is true that in xx the only erect full-length figures are in the middleground, so that our figures here as elsewhere are only approximate. The scenes by the St. Cecilia Master show a very small range of variation in the height of the figures: 56, 61, 61. Scene i (61 inches) once again conforms.

The distinctiveness of several parts of the *Legend* with respect to the number and height of the figures as well as the "intonaco style" is evident also in the pattern of color. The painter of Scenes xx–xxv employs in his preparation an unusual yellow and in his fresco an unusual violet. The luminous green of the St. Cecilia Master is distinctive. Further discussion of the color of these painters would, however, be of very limited value until the pigments they employed have been identified by chemical analysis. One pigment, however, makes its presence sufficiently clear quite without any analysis, and a comment about it may be useful. Cennino Cennini pointed out that white lead in mural paintings turns black, and it seems safe to suppose that where it was used in paintings on exterior walls exposed to moisture, the lead-carbonate-hydrate before long changed to lead sulphide in the presence of water and sulphide, and that certain dark, opaque surfaces in the frescoes are thus the consequence of the use of lead white.

White lead was used extensively by Cimabue and his followers. The painters of the *Legend* continued to employ the pigments, but more sparingly; its occurrence in the successive scenes of the cycle will be identified in the following chapter. In general it was used more in Scenes ii–xiii, and less on the south wall, beginning with Scene xvi. The St. Cecilia Master, whom we have characterized as an experienced mural painter, scarcely used the pigment at all, whether in Scene i or the three scenes on the south wall.

These observations prompt a general consideration. White lead was not employed in the Arena Chapel. And it is very little used in three frescoes (two Isaac scenes and the *Lamentation*) in the upper tier of frescoes in the Upper Church that are undubitably earlier than the *Legend* and are ascribed by many historians, including one of the two present writers, to Giotto. It appears in a highlight on a leg of the figure at the extreme right in the *Lamentation*, and in highlights on the hands of Isaac as Esau approaches him, though here the dark strips seem to have been rubbed down by a restorer. These facts bear on the problem of the attribution of the *Legend*, especially if the inclusion of the Isaac scenes in Giotto's oeuvre is correct. With respect to the use of white lead, the sequence would be:

1] Cimabue: extensive use.
2] Giotto (?), Isaac scenes and *Lamentation:* limited to a few highlights.
3] presumed Giotto, *Legend:* considerable use, especially in Scenes II–XIII, which are more frequently ascribed to Giotto. The lead, furthermore, is mixed with many colors and spread more broadly.
4] Giotto, Arena Chapel: none.
5] Giotto and associates, Bardi Chapel: none.[6]

The practice of the presumed Giotto appears erratic. Or is it rather the attributions?

NOTES

1. *A History of Painting in Italy*, first published 1864; ed. by L. Douglas, London, 1923, II, p. 14.
2. *The Mosaics of Norman Sicily*, London, 1949, p. 142. The scenes in question range from the Creation to Noah building the Ark.
3. Van Marle, *op. cit.*, III, pp. 284–285, supposed that the painter of Scenes I and XXVIII was "there at the beginning"; A. Smart, "The St. Cecilia Master and his School at Assisi," *Burlington Magazine*, CII, 1960, pp. 405–406.
4. C. Gnudi, *Giotto*, Milan, 1958, p. 66.
5. Procacci, *op. cit.*, pl. IX.
6. It would be premature to generalize about the use of white lead in post-Giottesque painting; the matter needs more extended study. Our impression is that it is used

sparingly, or not at all. From the floor of the chapels we recognize none in Maso's or Bernardo Daddi's frescoes in S. Croce, or in Nardo's in S. M. Novella. A scaffold in the Baroncelli Chapel has enabled us to identify a small amount in the fire on the altar of the temple in the *Expulsion of Joachim*, but otherwise none in Taddeo's entire cycle.

HEIGHT OF THE FIGURES IN THE CYCLE

Figures visible in full length and standing close to the picture plane were measured. Slight variations in posture, costume, and place in space make the measurements only approximately comparable. Scenes lacking in this list have no suitable figure.

Dimensions are given in centimeters and inches.

Scene	Height of Figure		Scene	Height of Figure	
I	156 cms.	61 ins.	XV	162 cms.	64 ins.
II	166 cms.	65 ins.	XVII	147 cms.	58 ins.
V	164 cms.	65 ins.	XVIII	147 cms.	58 ins.
VI	156 cms.	61.5 ins.	XX	146 cms.	58 ins.
VII	154 cms.	61 ins.	XXI	146 cms.	58 ins.
VIII	126 cms.	50 ins.	XXII	134 cms.	53 ins.
X	142 cms.	56 ins.	XXIII	140 cms.	55 ins.
XI	148 cms.	58 ins.	XXIV	135 cms.	53 ins.
XII	149 cms.	59 ins.	XXVI	156 cms.	61 ins.
XIII	154 cms.	61 ins.	XXVII	154 cms.	61 ins.
XIV	147 cms.	58 ins.	XXVIII	143 cms.	56 ins.

CHAPTER 3

The Evolution of a Fresco

Photographic illustration of progress in one
scene in the cycle may bring us closer to the thought of the painter
as he worked. The photographs disclose some of the realities of the
process of production and the kind of imaginative effort that they
stimulate.

The reader should perhaps be reminded of one or two things.
While interruption of the work during the execution of one patch
would have more or less undesirable consequences (the patch would
have to be finished *a secco*), technical considerations imposed no
limit on the duration of an interruption between patches. In our
series of reproductions, up to the last one, the blank white of the
paper always lies below the completed part of the fresco. The empty
paper is of course a symbol of the still unpainted rough plaster or
arriccio, and the reproductions therefore indicate that the *arriccio*
itself was bare. It is quite possible, however, that there was a sinopia
drawing on the *arriccio*, though no trace of one has yet been discovered on any exposed rough plaster in the cycle. (When asserting
that drawing on the *arriccio* is visible Toesca seems to us to mistake
the intonaco for the *arriccio*. See *Gli affreschi della Vita di San
Francesco nella Chiesa Superiore del Santuario di Assisi*, p. 13.)

If sinopia drawings existed we do not know of what kind. In such
a condition of ignorance it seemed to us more misleading to invent
a drawing, even schematically, than to create the impression that
there was none. If a sinopia was not used certainly a small drawing
served to establish the main elements of the design, and, as we have
argued above, such a small drawing probably represented the first
stage of composition in any case.

FIRST DAY

ON THE FIRST DAY the painter or painters began by executing in fresco the pink and white entablature over the scenes, not visible in the accompanying sequence of photographs but appearing in Fig. 15 (p. 46). Then they proceeded to the two capitals and the flat bands of red and green that frame the scenes. Finally they spread a gray watercolor over the "sky" as a preparation for azurite, which would be added *a secco* any time after the intonaco was dry.

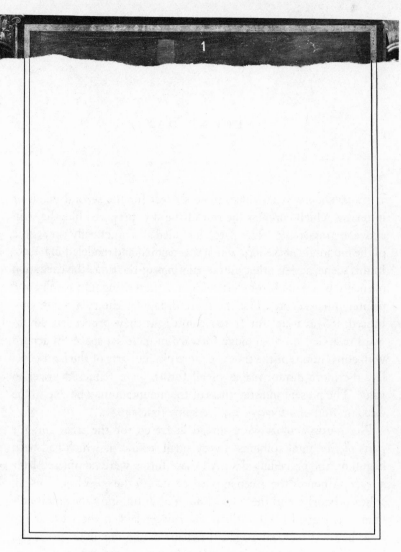

19. *The Miracle of the Spring*, first day. Assisi, S. Francesco.

SECOND DAY

THE SCAFFOLD WAS LOWERED some six feet for the second patch of intonaco, which contains the rest of the sky, prepared like the strip above in gray fresco. This patch included also practically the whole of the mountain at the left, which was painted and modeled in fresco. In this scene, and in other mural paintings of the time, the execution normally proceeded from left to right, as in writing. On patch 2 the painter thus executed first the more distant of the two mountains. Indeed, it was usual for fresco painters as they proceeded downward in actual space to move forward in pictorial space. In accord with conventions of the time the more distant parts of the landscape, like the more distant planes of all forms, were rendered lower in value. The present indistinctness of the mountain may be due to the discoloration of a fixative applied some time ago.

Preparatory colors were spread in fresco for the trees and for parts of the spiral columns, a very small section of which had been begun on the preceding day. All these forms were completed later *a secco*. Much of the green applied *a secco* to the trees has, as usual, adhered poorly, and the white lead used in finishing the spiral columns has turned black. When the painter laid in the trees at the right he must have envisaged the shape of the mountain precisely, because the trees grow out of it. Possibly he was guided by a sinopia drawing, but as we have said no trace of such drawings has yet been discovered. Extant sinopias, furthermore, concentrate on the figures, and rarely describe precise details of the setting.

20. *The Miracle of the Spring*, second day. Assisi, S. Francesco.

THIRD DAY

THE THIRD DAY WAS DEVOTED to the execution in fresco of the nearer, and therefore brighter, mountain. The painter also spread the fresco ground color of another section of the column at the right.

The progression down the wall, coupled with the peculiar nature of fresco, required that the painter have in mind a vivid and precise image of the *entire* scene when he began to paint at the top. Overpainting, to adjust a form in one of the first patches to one in a later patch, is not possible in fresco without excising the original intonaco and laying a fresh patch. Retouching would have to be done *a secco*, and this was usually limited to small areas. Some of the hands showing white lead in Scenes ii, v, and ix may have been retouched.

21. *The Miracle of the Spring*, third day. Assisi, S. Francesco.

FOURTH DAY

ONCE AGAIN the scaffold was lowered, down toward the lower border of the scene. Now that the painter had reached the heads of the figures, the size of his patch of intonaco contracted greatly. The heads and the rock behind them were painted in fresco. The intonaco for the column at the left was carried down a few feet, and the ground color was spread. It is notable that the heads of the friars, including one turned in an oblique position, were given final shape three days before the corresponding bodies.

22. *The Miracle of the Spring*, fourth day. Assisi, S. Francesco.

FIFTH DAY

THE FIFTH DAY WAS DEVOTED exclusively to the head of St. Francis, a limitation required not so much by his religious eminence or his centrality in the narrative as by the time consumed in working the halo in relief. A patch of plaster, much thicker than the normal layer of intonaco, was shaped in the form of a disk, and while it was still damp and soft, rays were indented in it by repeated applications of a specially shaped stick. The color in the head of St. Francis has not adhered well — not nearly so well as in the heads of the two friars. Since the surfaces around it are in good state, the poorer preservation of the saint's head is perhaps due to a delay in the painting, caused by the preparation of the halo. The colors, in other words, were applied after the carbonation of the lime in the intonaco was well advanced.

23. *The Miracle of the Spring*, fifth day. Assisi, S. Francesco.

SIXTH DAY

THE PAINTER, having just executed the head of the saint, decided to complete the figure before returning to the two friars. To the figure, which he could paint more broadly and rapidly than the head, he added the whole of the brightly lighted plane on which the saint kneels. He also prepared in fresco the two trees, later completed *a secco*.

24. *The Miracle of the Spring*, sixth day. Assisi, S. Francesco.

SEVENTH DAY

ON THIS PATCH the painter completed the two friars and the ass in front of them. All this he did in fresco, but afterwards for some reason he went over a small area of ground between the two hoofs in tempera, employing in his paint some white lead, which has since turned dark. The mottled surface of the shoulder of the friar at the left probably was caused by an altered fixative and the mountain above him may have been discolored by the same substance.

25. *The Miracle of the Spring*, seventh day. Assisi, S. Francesco.

EIGHTH DAY

THIS DAY WAS DEVOTED primarily to the man who drinks from the miraculous spring. Though the figure and the surrounding areas were painted in fresco, the colors have adhered imperfectly. The losses, especially in the face and the tunic, approximate those in the head of St. Francis. Did the intonaco in these areas dry faster than the painter expected? He may well have failed to take into account the consequences of the exceptional position of this scene. It is diagonally above a main door, and in the summer months, whenever the door was opened, it would be swept by a draught of dry rising warm air.

26. *The Miracle of the Spring,* eighth day. Assisi, S. Francesco.

NINTH DAY

THE SCAFFOLD WAS SET in its fourth and lowest position, two or three feet below the upper border of the simulated drapery underneath the scenes visible in Fig. 15 (p. 46). From this position the master painted in fresco the feet of the friars and the lowermost rocks. These rocks are also closest to the beholder, the last of four or five stages in the approach to the picture plane. On this day he also painted partly in fresco and partly *a secco* the lower border of the scene, the corbel table below it, and the upper part of the drapery (Fig. 16, p. 49).

27. *The Miracle of the Spring*, ninth day. Assisi, S. Francesco.

CHAPTER 4

The Twenty-eight Scenes

I

St. Francis Honored by a Simple Man of Assisi

THE PATTERN OF DIVISION of the area discloses an experienced and skillful fresco painter. The patches fall into four horizontal bands, which correspond no doubt to successively lower positions of the scaffold. With very few exceptions the joints coincide with the limits of large forms, which are often straight lines. (A dotted line such as appears in patch 10 signifies a suture that we judge may be present but which we could not actually discover.) The pattern exhibits therefore a general regularity and geometricity.

Most of the patches in this fresco are large. The execution in one day of an area as large and complex as 2, with its palace, its tympanum containing two Victories, and its *cosmati* frieze implies an impressive mastery of fresco technique. Almost all the scene was painted in true fresco. The blue azurite background or "sky" was, as always, painted *a secco*. The cloak of St. Francis, likewise blue, was laid *a secco* over a gray fresco preparation, as in Scenes II and III. As a consequence of a change of design or a miscalculation, the lower right edge of the cloak was not contained in patch 6. It was completed *a secco* on patches 7 and 13.

The data provided by overlapping are not sufficient to establish the order in which two patches such as 3 and 4 were executed. Convenience suggests that the present 3 was laid and painted before 4 because the platform used for 2 certainly extended the width of the scene. The possibility remains however that 4 might have been painted before 3. We cannot see that such a reversal would be significant.

A haloed head was frequently painted on a separate circular patch because the preparation of the plaster, which was raised in relief and then impressed with rays, was time-consuming. Patch 5 is no excep-

28. St. Cecilia Master, Scene 1, *St. Francis Honored by a Simple Man of Assisi.*
Assisi, S. Francesco.

tion to this practice. 12 is separate also, no doubt because the narrative culminates in the dramatic exchange between this carefully studied head and that of St. Francis. The heads of the two citizens of Assisi behind St. Francis were painted in one day, together with a section of the palace. The corresponding patch at the right includes only one head; the other (9) has been isolated on a separate patch (Fig. 28a). This head constitutes then a special case in the fresco. Perhaps it was singled out for more careful execution because it refers to a particular person or, more likely, because it is peculiarly expressive. Of the faces of the four bystanders this is the most emotional.

The man's features are strikingly individualized. His eyes are so closely set they are unusual even among the other figures in the frescoes of the St. Cecilia Master. His brows are knitted, his cheeks furrowed, his lips drawn down, so that he seems to scowl rather than convey simple astonishment. His companion is severe, while the two men behind the saint are milder and even gay of mien, but perhaps a little sanctimonious. Did the painter intend to polarize these two groups, as the designer of Scene v, St. Francis confronting his father, clearly did? The followers of the saint on one side, his opponents, wearing peaked caps, on the other? There is no warrant for such a differentiation in Bonaventura's *Legend*, but Christian iconography in general could provide many models.

The gray rectangle extending downward from the column of the temple just in front of St. Francis shows the condition of the surface before the cycle was cleaned in the late 'thirties.

28a. *Head of a man* (detail of Scene 1).
Assisi, S. Francesco.

II

St. Francis Gives His Cloak to a Poor Knight

THE PATTERN OF PATCHES is less geometric than in Scene 1, but this difference is due in part to the less geometric design of the fresco itself. The divisions usually coincide with the large forms. To this principle there are, in the figure of the knight, small but probably significant exceptions. His hand, part of his foot, and even the edge of his skirt extend onto the adjacent patch 8. On the other hand his dress does not quite reach the suture between 9 and 10. The obvious inference is that the painter revised his intention after spreading the intonaco, and shifted the figure a little to the left.

There is much more *a secco* painting than in 1. As in the preceding scene, the tunic of St. Francis was finished in blue tempera, most of which has come away, leaving the gray fresco preparation. But in Scene II white lead, applied with other pigments *a secco*, is employed rather extensively. "It is even used on walls," Cennino says in chapter 59 of his treatise, "but avoid it as much as you can for in time it turns black." Precisely this it has done in the hands of the saint and the visible hand of the knight, making the reproduction of the latter in particular look like a photographic negative.

The St. Cecilia Master avoided the use of white lead in this way, but the painter of Scene II employed it in other larger areas. There is much of it in the front face of the terrain along the lower frame, so that originally the contrast between it and the lighted plane above was not nearly so great as it is now. Still more conspicuous is the altered surface of the horse. This has been greatly affected both by the peeling of the tempera pigments and the darkening of the white lead in them. The changes in the surface of the horse and of the tunic of the saint have fundamentally disturbed the coloristic effect of this fresco.

The saddle of the horse, prepared in red-brown fresco, was finished in a similar reddish tempera, which has adhered imperfectly. The pommels, in yellow tempera, have scaled off entirely, leaving only the outlines. Of the reins, likewise painted *a secco* over the frescoed terrain, only traces remain. Where the tempera has peeled along the edges of the horse, the yellow outlines are visible. The blue tempera of the poor knight's cap has flaked, accidentally making him look more shabby than the painter intended.

The mode of executing the azurite tunic of St. Francis conforms to Cennino's prescription. "If you would make a mantle . . . of azure only," he says in chapter 83, "first lay in fresco a ground . . . of sinopia and black [in Scenes i–iii the ground is gray] . . . having previously marked out the finished drawing of folds with an iron point or needle . . ." Incisions for this purpose are visible in the tunic of the saint.

It is possible, but not probable, that the order of executing patches 5 and 6 was the reverse of the one given on the diagram.

29. Scene II, *St. Francis Gives His Cloak to a Poor Knight.* Assisi, S. Francesco.

III

The Vision of the Palace and Armor

THIS FRESCO is much less well preserved than the first two. In the left half even some areas finished in fresco, such as the head of Christ, or the framework of the bed below the saint's feet, have suffered, no doubt from water. Most of the ornamental motifs on the curtains have been lost. The blue tempera on the tunic of St. Francis has disintegrated. It has fallen away also on the mantle of Christ, and with it has gone almost all of the gold striation, which throughout the cycle marks supernatural figures. In the castle the flags and the armor were painted first in a red fresco. The patterns were then developed in tempera, and are only partly preserved.

Patch 7 contains not only the head of the saint but his shoulders as well. The painter apparently decided to add the shoulders to the head and the halo — usually a day's work by themselves — because there was much detail in adjacent patch 8 and because only the underpainting of the shoulders was in fresco. The shoulders could be finished in tempera at leisure.

The reason for the curious triangle in the suture between patches 2 and 3 is not clear.

30. Scene III, *The Vision of the Palace and Armor*. Assisi, S. Francesco.

IV

St. Francis Praying in S. Damiano

IN THIS SCENE, which is damaged all along the left side, there is only one building and one large figure, so that the pattern of divisions is simple and regular. Each of the larger forms falls for the most part within one patch, but there are minor exceptions, as in the preceding scenes, which suggest either that some shapes had not been established carefully and precisely before the intonaco was spread, or that a slight change was made as the painting began. Thus only a small part of the dark red molding on the base of the building is included in patch 3; the rest is in 6. This uneconomical division was abandoned in patches 4 and 5, which include all of the molding.

It is notable that the normal left-to-right sequence does not appear in the lower zone. The middle patch (5) was painted after the farther one (4), perhaps because, when portraying the response of the saint to Christ on the cross, the painter wished to have Christ in being. This motive would have been more compelling, of course, if there were no sinopia drawing on the *arriccio*. The altar and the architecture in patch 4 were painted in fresco whereas the detailed forms of the cross were developed more slowly in tempera. Almost all of this tempera has fallen away, exposing the yellow drawing. There are traces of gold below the loincloth, and of white lead, now black, in the Virgin and St. John. White lead was used also in the body of Christ.

Unless we are mistaken the halo and head of St. Francis are in the same patch as his body. His tunic was, of course, finished in blue tempera, so that only the preparatory color needed to be laid in while the plaster was damp. The blue tunic is not prepared in gray, like the tunic in the preceding frescoes or, indeed, the half-dome in this scene, but in a clear red earth. The outlines are reddish yellow.

31. Scene IV, *St. Francis Praying in S. Damiano*. Assisi, S. Francesco.

St. Francis Renouncing His Father

IN THIS SCENE, the first with numerous figures, the painter has combined many heads on one patch. It is however true, especially in the first of these patches (4), that the painting did not quite keep pace with the drying of the plaster, and the colors adhered imperfectly as a result. Parts of 5 have deteriorated also. Curiously, the small patch 8 contains very little fresco; even the hand was painted *a secco*. The feet in eleven were added *a secco* also.

Azurite applied *a secco* has flaked off the following areas: in 13, the mantle held around the saint and the bishop's mantle; the tunic in 8; the cloth, prepared in rose, over the arm of the father in 12. The dark cloth over his arm was painted in tempera with much white lead, now nearly black, and a similar technique was used for the hand of the friar at the extreme right. Perhaps the lead was used in the hand to correct a color that appeared to require it only after drying.

32. Scene v, *St. Francis Renouncing His Father.* Assisi, S. Francesco.

The Vision of Innocent III

THIS IS THE FIRST SCENE in which the figure of St. Francis is well preserved, because he has now exchanged his blue tunic for the brown Franciscan habit, which can be painted in fresco. The left half of his skirt, however, has darkened strangely, probably because of the addition of white lead. His foot was not included in the same patch as his body, whether purposely or because of oversight or an alteration of the design. It was added on patch 10 in tempera, and the white lead in it has turned black.

The painter's decision about the three figures at the right is interesting. Patches 6 and 9 each contain an entire figure (we were, at least, unable to find sutures within them), whereas the head of the guard at the right, on 7, has been isolated on a separate patch (Fig. 33*a*). This head, then, received more attention than that of the Pope. Indeed it is less conventional and, with its rich interplay of light and dark, more expressive. It is represented in the more complex three-quarters position, whereas the Pope is frontal and the other watcher in full profile. Here, as in Scene 1, the division of the surface proves to be a barometer of the degree of the painter's concern. It is evident that its rise and fall does not always coincide with hierarchical considerations. A subordinate figure from the religious point of view may engage the painter because of its human or aesthetic possibilities.

The spatial structure of the scene has been weakened by the disappearance of a piece of furniture, a sort of *cassone*, between the watchers and the bed in 8 and 9. It was painted in tempera. Three of the four statues on the roof were also painted in tempera; only the red fresco drawing remains. The color in the fourth at the left, however, is preserved; it is yellow, simulating gold (Fig. 33*b*).

33. Scene VI, *The Vision of Innocent* III. Assisi, S. Francesco.

33a. Head of a watcher (detail of Scene VI).

33*b*. *Statue* (detail of Scene VI).

VII

Innocent III Approves the Rule of the Order

THE INTERIOR of the papal chamber was originally even richer than it appears today, for some of the ornament applied *a secco* on the hanging has been lost, and almost all of the pattern of the carpet on the floor. In the carpet there were large confronted birds, traces of which are still visible here and there. Details such as the design of the crown of the Pope's tiara were, as usual, added *a secco*, and are poorly preserved.

It is notable that in the group at the right the usual left-to-right sequence was interrupted and the head of the Pope, who is also a main actor, was painted before the bishop to the left of him. At the left there is an odd division: patch 5 has no less than seven heads, though each is not fully visible, while 7 has little more than two hands.

34. Scene VII, *Innocent* III *Approves the Rule of the Order.* Assisi, S. Francesco.

VIII

The Vision of the Fiery Chariot

THIS SCENE, painted almost entirely in *buon fresco* except for the blue ground, is one of the best preserved in the cycle. Much of the gilt striation on the habit of the saint, who here appears "transfigured, like a second Elijah," according to Bonaventura, is lost, and the gilt in the rays emanating from his body has likewise peeled. In the relatively large patch 7 the face and hand of the sleeping friar have suffered losses, no doubt because the finishing touches were applied to these carefully studied forms after the intonaco had become quite dry. The similar head and hand in 9, painted afterward, were separated from the surrounding area, and they are very much better preserved. Perhaps 9 was actually redone on a patch that replaced the original, which in that case would have been cut out.

Patch 3 is exceptional, including as it does the saint as well as part of a building. The joint between the head or body of the saint and the rest of this patch may be so smooth as to have escaped our attention. But this patch may actually be the first specimen of a trend towards larger patches and the unification of the figures, even of St. Francis, on one intonaco section. Similar large divisions appear in the two following frescoes. If there actually is no joint within patch 3, the size of the patch, with of course the subsequent penetration of moisture, may account for the poor adherence of much color in the head of the saint.

In patch 13 the hand of the friar was finished *a secco*, with the admixture of the usual lead white, now black. The bases of the piers were finished with lead white also.

35. Scene VIII, *The Vision of the Fiery Chariot*. Assisi, S. Francesco.

IX

The Vision of the Thrones in Heaven

THE DIVISIONS OF THIS SCENE are large and logical, and they testify to the self-assurance of the painter. The entire figure of St. Francis appears once again to be within one patch. The blue background around his figure did not increase the pressure on the painter because it was, of course, finished in tempera. Still, the consequences of undertaking in one day an entire haloed figure may perhaps be seen in the state of preservation of the head compared to that of the friar, which is on a separate patch (Figs. 36a, 36b). This poorer adhesion of the head of the saint has occurred, furthermore, despite the fact that the hands were not finished while the intonaco was wet. The surface, now ruinous, consists of a color that contains white lead, instead of the lime white or *bianco sangiovanni* used in fresco.

The division of the intonaco in the figures of the friar and the saint seems to reverse the usual practice. Perhaps this reversal is due to the fact that while the saint prays quietly, according to the *Legend*, in an abandoned church, the friar sees the thrones in heaven and the angel, who informs him that the most splendid seat is reserved for the saint. His face is livelier than that of St. Francis, and richer in expressive nuances.

The body and wings of the angel may be on the same patch that includes much of the background. Though the red tunic and green mantle of the angel were painted in *buon fresco*, the gold striation and the hands and feet were finished *a secco*. In its present condition the apse approximates Bonaventura's description of it as "delapidated" far more than in its original state, when the lantern, now reduced to the red drawing, glistened in silver and the cross, rising above a golden base, shone with a similar color. The front of the altar was covered with a rich red pattern while the apse presented a quiet blue below vibrant green and black coffers in the ceiling.

36. Scene ix, *The Vision of the Thrones in Heaven.* Assisi, S. Francesco.

36a. Head of St. Francis (detail of Scene ix).

36b. Head of a friar (detail of Scene IX).

X

Expulsion of the Devils from Arezzo

THE DIVISIONS RESEMBLE those in the preceding fresco. The entire figure of St. Francis was again painted on one patch, though all of it was in *buon fresco*. Friar Silvester, too, likewise all in fresco, was painted on one patch, with the exception of the feet. It was possible on the other hand for the painter to produce in one day, in fresco, an entire flock of anthropomorphic devils as well as a half-dozen towers. To be sure the devils, while highly individualized (they symbolize factional strife), are more summarily painted than the friars.

37. Scene x, *Expulsion of the Devils from Arezzo*. Assisi, S. Francesco.

XI

The Proof by Fire

THE FIRE SEEMS to have been painted on a separate patch, although we could not be certain of a joint along the right side. An object of this size was normally included with other forms, and the painter may have decided to isolate it because of its position between two levels of the scaffold, and perhaps also because fire was not frequently represented in the painting of the time and required special attention. The fire was originally more vivid than it is now. The outer flames, especially those added on patch 3, were painted on dry intonaco, and they have adhered imperfectly.

Most of the forms are painted in *buon fresco*, but the colors, especially in the faces, have not survived as well as in some other frescoes. The technical decline is accompanied by an artistic one; the figures in patches 4, 8, and 9 are especially weak.

The green festoons held by the four winged "putti" on the finials above are no longer clearly visible. The little winged figures, like the lions on the base of the sultan's throne, were painted with a viscous emulsion of gilt, and then shaded with parallel or hatched lines in black (Figs. 38*a*, 38*b*). This layer of gilt has not of course adhered well to the plaster. Its disappearance has laid bare the yellow drawing for these forms. The nature of this drawing, free and searching, indicates that the precise shapes of these figures and even of the base of the throne were not previously fixed.

The gilt in the halo of St. Francis has similarly peeled. Disclosure of the intonaco has made visible random brush strokes of various colors (Fig. 38*c*). The painters, knowing that the halo would be gilded, wiped their brushes on the intonaco as they worked on surfaces nearby.

38. Scene XI, *The Proof by Fire*. Assisi, S. Francesco.

38a. *Statue of a putto*
(detail of Scene

In this fresco, as in many others, there are many small indentations spaced at intervals, usually along a straight line. They are the marks left by nails or pins set in the plaster, from which strings were stretched. They normally occur in large geometric forms, and in this scene they are especially clear along the molding in patch 3. Here as elsewhere small changes were made in the painting, for the line established by the pins does not coincide with any of the lines of the molding. It is noteworthy that we could not find corresponding holes in the base of the sultan's throne, and the yellow drawing for this base, full of trials and corrections, suggests that the shapes were worked out freehand on the intonaco.

38b. *Statue of a putto* (detail of Scene XI).

38c. *Head of St. Francis* (detail of Scene XI).

XII

The Transfiguration

THE COLOR PAINTED in fresco as a preparation for the blue of the background varies from patch to patch in this fresco, as in the others. The shade of gray, whether lighter or darker, seems to depend upon the color readily available to the painter at the moment — what, in other words, he happens to have in his paint bowls. This difference of preparation, never intended to be visible, together with the varying adherence of the azurite from one patch to another, produces the kind of crazy-quilt pattern that we see in sections 1, 2, 3, 7, 8, and 11 in this scene. To this variety a chemical change contributes also. When subjected to sufficient moisture blue azurite changes into green malachite — a common change that may be observed, for instance, at the extreme right in patch 2.

The six arcs of heaven above Christ were originally in a regularly graduated series, the lightest of them nearest Christ. Of most of them, little but the preparatory grays are now visible. The garment of Christ, like that of other supernatural figures, was striated in gold. This figure is weak; the hand is remarkably boneless and feeble, executed by a painter who had little sense of structure and volume (Fig. 39a). The hands of St. Francis are, on the contrary, not only on separate patches and carefully painted — probably on the same day, as we have indicated by giving them the same number — but by a better master (Fig. 39b). There is even a difference of color — the author of the hand of Christ tries to compensate for his anxious, niggling definition and weak structure by a hot, declamatory, orange-red color.

White lead was used extensively in the lighted areas of the habit in 11, in the lowest part of the cloud in 8, and along the lower outline of the saint.

39. Scene XII, *The Transfiguration*. Assisi, S. Francesco.

39a. Hand of Christ (detail of Scene XII).

39b. Hand of St. Francis (detail of Scene XII).

XIII

The Miracle at Greccio

THIS SCENE CONTAINS many more figures than the preceding frescoes. Three, four, or more heads are painted in one day. Among the heads, more than one style is clearly visible, as in Scene XI, and the weakest painter again worked at the extremities. His presence is especially evident in patch 15 (Fig. 40b), but the superiority of the singing friar to those just below leads us to believe that the singer was actually on a separate patch, though we did not detect the join.

Only one head is certainly isolated on a separate patch — 9 (Fig. 40a). This friar sings more passionately than any other and he has indeed often been singled out for superior vigor. The difference between this head and others seems to be due not only to the longer time available for its execution, but to the intervention of a superior artist. His mastery shows itself in a more incisive drawing and a firmer structure. His individuality is evident also in the fine network of lines, the telling cross-hatching (absent from the other heads), and the more naturalistic smaller forms, such as the teeth and the ear, which are unmatched in any of the other heads. It is a notable fact that here again, as in Scene VI, the best painter at work on the fresco singled out for special treatment a head interesting for its position or action rather than its religious significance.

Though most of the scene is in true fresco and rather well preserved, some forms executed in tempera have undergone basic alteration. Both the ox and the four columns of the ciborium, now very dark, were originally high in value because of the presence of much lead white (Fig. 40c). The mantle of the layman in patch 13, now light gray, was originally blue, most of which has disappeared. The mantle of the man in patch 16 was also originally blue, but we see now only the exceptionally vigorous broad strokes of the preparation in gray.

40. Scene XIII, *The Miracle at Greccio*. Assisi, S. Francesco.

40a. *Friars* (detail of Scene XIII).

40b. *Heads of Friars* (detail of Scene XIII).

There are four groups of candles, but only those on the pulpit were foreseen, or at least prepared, from the beginning. The azurite of the background was not carried over the spaces occupied by these candles, so that where the ocher tempera in which they were painted has fallen away the outline drawing on the bare intonaco is visible. The small candles on the lectern in patch 6 were added in a yellowish tempera which has adhered to the white of the wall but not to the blue of the background. The two candles at both sides of the crucifix were added in tempera without any preparation, and they are scarcely visible now.

40c. *Ciborium* (detail of Scene XIII).

SCENE XIV, *The Miracle of the Spring*, is discussed at length in the preceding chapter (Figs. 19–27).

XV

Preaching to the Birds

THIS FRESCO, like XIV, is on the east or entrance wall, just beside and above a door, and it may have been affected by the draughts and rapid changes of temperature that damaged XIV.

The effectiveness of this scene is disturbed by extreme differences in the state of preservation of the background. In patches 1 and 6 much of the azurite is preserved, in patch 2 almost none, and in the two small patches, 8, almost all. The crowns of the trees, rather weak in shape, are peculiarly gray-green in color. The yellow lights, furthermore, have not adhered to the green.

The birds in patch 6 were mostly finished in tempera. They have adhered very much less well to the azurite than to the ocher terrain. (The phenomenon is similar to the candles in the lectern in Scene XIII.) They have adhered relatively well also to the tree trunk and to the rock below it, which was originally light in color but, because of white lead, has blackened.

This is one of the frescoes that present alternatives in the sequence of patches. 3 underlies 4 and 5, 5 underlies 6 and 7, so that the head of St. Francis, rather than the habit of the friar, might have been painted immediately after the head of the friar.

The hands of St. Francis are on separate small patches, as in Scene XII. In the *Preaching* we have been able to ascertain that the intonaco of these small oval patches overlaps the adjacent intonaco on all sides. The original hands were perhaps cut out and replaced by the present ones.

41. Scene xv, *Preaching to the Birds*. Assisi, S. Francesco.

XVI

The Death of the Knight of Celano

THIS SCENE CONTAINS about as many figures and as many patches as the *Miracle at Greccio* opposite it. Indeed one of the more readily identifiable painters of the *Miracle*, whose curved eyes and mouths are visible in patch 15, seems to have worked in patch 11 in this scene. This patch, containing a dozen heads, is exceptionally large.[1] We suspect the existence of one or more internal divisions, but we were unable to find them. On the other hand, the most intent head, and the one in most complex perspective (because inclined down and toward the right) are on separate patches (13, 14).

The scene, executed mostly in fresco, is well preserved. Azurite has, as usual, scaled off, exposing gray preparation in the figures at the extreme left and right of patch 15. White lead in the fish on the table and in numerous utensils has turned them black. The loss that affects the design of the fresco most is the molding that extended across the rear wall behind the head of the saint and helped to fix him firmly in space. It is clearly visible on the front faces of the posts, having adhered well to the yellow pigment, though the white lead "lights" are now dark. Very little is left on the brown wall behind except the red outlines.

1. Borsook, *op. cit.*, p. 130 observed that in the *Last Judgment* in the Arena Chapel fifteen of the Blessed behind Scrovegni are on one patch. The one figure of Scrovegni, on the other hand, is on four patches.

42. Scene XVI, *The Death of the Knight of Celano*. Assisi, S. Francesco.

XVII

St. Francis Preaching before Honorius III

THIS IS THE FIRST, and only, fresco in the entire cycle in which every head is on a separate patch. These patches, furthermore, are all quite small except for 9. This difference would give us the key to the exceptional pattern of divisions did we not already divine it in the subject represented. For 9 contains the head of a Franciscan seated on the floor whereas all the smaller patches, apart from the special case of the saint, contain the heads of the Pope and, as the *Legenda Maior* says, members of the curia. It was, then, the ecclesiastical importance of the persons represented that led the painter to decide to paint them more slowly and with greater care. He may have intended to refer to contemporary clerics; the frescoes were part of a program of embellishment of S. Francesco that had papal support.

The richness of the Gothic hall extends to such details as the nails that support the hanging, which originally shone with gold. After executing the great arcade, or perhaps even after executing the entire scene, the painter decided the hall was still not sufficiently rich and the horizontal line above too stark, so he cut out the original intonaco and added three splendid leafy ornaments (4).

The red mantle of the figure at the extreme right is only preparation, and the same must be said of much of the blue habit of the friar seated on the bench just in front of St. Francis. The columns are dark because of the white lead in them.

43. Scene XVII, *St. Francis Preaching before Honorius* III. Assisi, S. Francesco.

XVIII

The Appearance at Arles

THIS FRESCO, which is stylistically related to the preceding *Preaching*, shows a similar mosaic. There are, however, three patches containing two heads (20, 22, 25), and one containing three (23). There was, furthermore, more technical reason for isolating heads in this fresco than in the one preceding because there the bodies or draperies of three figures could be finished later in tempera whereas here every figure was painted entirely in fresco.

The disappearance of the gilt on the halo of St. Francis has disclosed yellow drawings; free, rapid definitions of head and tunic outside the final painted area (Fig. 44*a*). While we could not trace the lower boundary of patch 8 it seems probable that the waistline and sleeve of the saint were altered after the intonaco was laid.

On the rear wall, to the left of each of the three arches or brackets that support the ceiling, there is a patch of shadow. These shadows, laid over all the colors but apparently authentic, are graduated in value, the darker part containing more black, the lighter more umber. At their widest they are about one foot across, wider than they would need to be if they were intended only to separate the plane of the bracket from that of the wall. The lower edge of each, furthermore, repeats the curvature of the bracket. It is difficult to escape the conclusion that they are meant to be cast shadows. They would not, furthermore, be the only primordial specimens of these luminary phenomena in the cycle, as we shall shortly see.

44*a*. *Head of St. Francis*
(detail of Scene XVIII).

44. Scene XVIII, *The Appearance at Arles*. Assisi, S. Francesco.

XIX

The Stigmatization

THIS BEAUTIFUL FRESCO has deteriorated rather differently from preceding scenes. In patch 3 too large and complex a surface, including a raised halo, seems to have been attempted, and the advanced carbonation left much of the pigment free to fall away. While the surface around the head of St. Francis is rather well preserved his face has lost much of its color. And although the lower-right corner of the scene has been generally damaged by humidity its effect is scarcely sufficient to account for the complete disappearance of the color in the face of the reading friar. Only the yellow preparation remains. The condition of this head is characteristic of the frescoes in the next bay.

The style of the friar confirms this relationship, and it is evident that the chief painter of the frescoes of the next two bays began to work in *The Stigmatization*, the last of the four frescoes in the first bay on this wall. The head of the friar is entirely his, and he very probably helped in the execution of other areas, such as the seraph and the exceptionally delicate saint. They show more or less clearly the softer textures, the finely graduated modeling, and the suffused light of the following bays.

From the bare rocks just below St. Francis a few small plants grow and flower (Fig. 45a). They represent no doubt a beautiful culmination in nature comparable to that of the spirit in the space just above. The painter's affectionate portrayal of the curling movement and the delicate life of these little plants proves to us as clearly as anything in these frescoes that a new era in the history of art has begun. They have a numerous progeny in the fifteenth and later centuries. The blue flower reproduced was painted *a secco* over the

45. Scene XIX, *The Stigmatization*. Assisi, S. Francesco.

45a. *Flower* (detail of Scene XIX).

frescoed rocks, after they had dried. The outlines of these complex forms turning in space are defined with an assurance and precision that imply a model drawn on some other surface.

XX

The Death of St. Francis

AS WE PROCEED to examine the cycle we recognize stylistic and technical variations from fresco to fresco and also within the frescoes, but apart from the difference between Scene I and Scene II the greatest change we have observed begins with *The Death of St. Francis*. The stylistic novelty of this and the following scenes has been observed before; the pattern of divisions of the intonaco makes it strikingly clear.

The designer of the scene has elected to introduce more than forty witnesses of the death of the saint or of the rise of his soul to heaven. In the lowest of the three zones into which the scene is divided friars who had been close to the saint mourn his passing from the world. Above them other Franciscans have gathered for the ceremony of the obsequies, and in the uppermost zone the soul of St. Francis, not a "luminous star" as Bonaventura says but a diminutive saint showing his wounds, ascends to the region of "light and peace" surrounded by a bevy of angels.

Contrary to the *Legend*, only one friar seems to observe his rise, just as very few of the standing friars look down at the dead body. Though the fresco is difficult to read because of its design and its present state, the three main zones are remarkably independent of each other. They correspond, as we observed earlier, to three platforms of the scaffold. Contemplating these facts one is led to suppose that the painter had not had much experience with compositions on this scale. One begins to imagine him working on each of his platforms, exceptionally engrossed with the painting immediately before him and exceptionally mindless of the rest of the scene, above or below. Of course this reference of compositional peculiarities to actual working conditions would be less meaningful if the painter was guided by a rather detailed small drawing or a similarly detailed sinopia. Perhaps, however, one or the other or both were summary, allowing the master to develop the zonal integrity to which we have referred.

There are, in any event, other reasons to suppose that the painter had not worked much previously in large scale on the wall, or at least in fresco. For one thing, he approached the task of execution more hesitantly, and he seems to have worked more slowly. The scene has an unprecedented number of figures; several times those in any preceding fresco. To accommodate them the painter has placed most of them at some distance in space, so that their actual size would be considerably reduced. He judged it necessary, however, to give to these smaller figures approximately the same amount of time allotted to larger ones in preceding frescoes. Indeed, the consistent practice of painting only one mantle in a day, as in the series 31 to 40, is unprecedented in the cycle.

Other signs of inexperience in fresco painting may perhaps be seen in the sequence of patches. In a few of the preceding scenes the usual direction of work from left to right is, as we have seen, interrupted and reversed for special reasons in one or two patches. In the *Death*, however, an entire series of patches, from 18 through 25, was produced from right to left. Lack of a regular procedure may be seen also in other parts of the scene. Could the painter have been left-handed, or ambidextrous?

Throughout the fresco, furthermore, the draperies of the figures are better preserved than the heads. Even where a head was executed on a separate patch, as in numbers 22 and 41, little but the preparation is left. This preparation is itself distinctive, consisting of a yellow line, or rather an orange-yellow wash, with which the painter evokes a remarkably mobile countenance bathed in a soft light and transparent shadows (Fig. 46*a*).

Why so much of the paint in the heads has disappeared entirely, exposing this yellow preparation, is not entirely clear. No doubt the working habits of the painter are no less responsible than his pigments or vehicle. Perhaps he employed an oily substance in the preparation that prevented a tight incorporation of the overlying

46. Scene xx, *The Death of St. Francis*. Assisi, S. Francesco.

46a. Friars (detail of Scene xx).

pigments. Perhaps he proceeded with such deliberation that the intonaco became too dry while he was still painting. Certainly he demanded an exceptionally fine, flat intonaco. The joints were smoothed over with great care, leaving a scarcely perceptible difference of level. As a consequence the joints in this fresco were far more difficult to find than in any preceding fresco. They are in fact exceptional in this respect among all the frescoes of the time. The sequence in Scene xx was equally difficult to ascertain, and the number of our errors, especially of omission, is no doubt higher than in other scenes.

It is noteworthy that the painter who brings his intonaco to such a state of refinement shows exceptional subtlety in the painting itself.

He delights in the rendition of textures, especially in the soft silkiness of draperies, and in this respect, as well as with regard to the design of the folds and of the figures he seems to have studied carefully the Isaac scenes at the upper level in the church or other works of their painter. Though he strives for monumental effects, as in the great stocky figures in 35 and 36 with their huge sleeves, he is more a painter of complex, luminous surfaces than of volume and mass. And his colors, in which violets and purples predominate, promote and enrich these effects. He uses a resonant mixture of red and black in the habit of the friar in patch 47. And he delights in effects of transparency, as in patch 33, where the yellow underpainting shines through the white overlay.

The nature of the art and of the technique of this painter suggests that he worked normally on panel and that his prior experience on the wall was very limited. He was more accustomed, in other words, to a much smaller scale, to an absolutely smooth gesso, and to a slower pace of execution. His subtleties of color and surface would be, perhaps, more telling in an altarpiece than in a mural. He is, in any event, one of the three most distinctive and impressive masters of the cycle. He must in fact have been one of the prominent painters of the time, closely related to the St. Cecilia Master but independent of him. Perhaps some day his style will be identified in panel painting.

The garments of the angels as well as of the ascending figure of St. Francis were striated, as usual in the cycle. The disc around the bust of the saint was originally blue, shot with red rays.

XXI

The Visions of Friar Augustine and of the Bishop of Assisi

THOUGH THIS FRESCO is much simpler in design than xx, and in general better preserved, its present state resembles its predecessor in one significant respect. Once again many heads, or at least faces, have lost almost all of their paint, and once again the orange-yellow shading is exposed. Similarly the draperies painted in fresco are, as in xx, very much better preserved.

What was executed *a secco*, such as the habit of the standing friar in patch 13, has as usual deteriorated. The light-gray forms in the hanging behind the bishop represent the preparation for a vanished blue. In places this blue has turned to malachite. Similarly the bishop's mantle consists largely of the red preparation for dark blue, and the now much-too-insistent bedcover was modeled in green, most of which is lost. The vault and the dome were originally the usual blue.

The joints in the very smooth intonaco are again carefully masked, and it may be that an internal division in 4 and perhaps also in 2 has escaped us. The composition as a whole was not conducive to the kind of tripartite horizontal division that was so basic to the design of the preceding fresco. The composition of xxi is more unified, perhaps because of increasing experience, but the inability or unwillingness to integrate the whole, at least formally, is still evident. The relationship of the bishop's chamber to Augustine's church is rather awkward.

It is noteworthy that, of the two similar visions, Augustine's is given so much more prominence than the bishop's. Here the Order asserts itself, preferring a friar to a person of higher ecclesiastical rank.

47. Scene XXI, *The Visions of Friar Augustine and of the Bishop of Assisi.*
Assisi, S. Francesco.

XXII

Obsequies and the Testimony of Jerome

LIKE XX, this is a populous scene, though the number of figures is less. There are, however, far fewer patches — twenty compared with fifty-four. The draperies of two or three figures are more often now on one patch, and the master has painted many more heads in a day. It seems probable that we have failed to discover an internal division in 6, and possibly also in 8, but the greater speed and confidence of the painter in his third fresco would be evident in any event. The colors, notably in the faces, have adhered somewhat better (Fig. 48a), apart from the section at the right that has been ruined entirely by a greater penetration of water. Some of this area was, furthermore, finished *a secco:* notably the frontal figure in 20, and his hand in 19, now partly black because of the use of lead.

Patch 2, containing two images as well as the dome and the rood beam, is large, but much of the painting was done after the intonaco had dried. Both the *Madonna* and the *Crucifix* now consist to a large extent only of the characteristic orange-yellow "wash" and some terra verde shading. The rood beam was executed in fresco, but the distant wall of the church was not, and it has become, therefore, a ghostly building. A string course just below the rood beam descends slowly from the left into the capital of the pier supporting the arch of the dome. This pier extends downward at approximately the center of the scene. The arch was originally brown, around a blue dome.

This is the last of three scenes in the bay, but the painter has sought to give the impression that the images on the rood beam were seen from a position far to the right, near the piers dividing this bay from the next. The right sides of the objects are invariably visible, and in the case of the *Madonna* several wooden struts behind the

48. Scene XXII, *Obsequies and the Testimony of Jerome*. Assisi, S. Francesco.

137

48a. *Friars* (detail of Scene XXII).

panel are in clear view. All of the images seem to incline forward into the nave, like the crucifix in Scene XIII, which is seen from the back. The present tilted axes of the images may not however represent the painter's first intention. An original drawing still clearly visible at close range above the Madonna fixes the apex of the panel over the far-right corner of the drapery behind the Virgin. If the verticals of the panel rose perpendicularly from the rood beam the apex would fall in precisely this point.

XXIII

St. Clare Grieving over the Body of St. Francis
at S. Damiano

THIS SCENE, the first in a bay, has much in common with XXII, the last scene in the preceding bay. The related compositions, involving the body of St. Francis attended by a crowd while a large structure rises at the right, are partly responsible for the similar patterns of patches. But a very similar personal choice is evident also, for instance, in the long bands of heads in both frescoes. The pattern of division of the intonaco confirms the close stylistic relationship, of which a conspicuous symptom is the unusual and very prominent figure seen from the back in the left part of both scenes.

The technique and the color are very close to the scenes in the preceding bay. As in those scenes the painter has smoothed the joints with the greatest care, and we may have failed to detect a few of them. Patch 4, like 6 in XXII, is exceptionally long, and there may be a division within 21. The flesh colors in this fresco, however, have not fallen off as in the preceding bay. Perhaps the painter had gained experience and worked more rapidly; or he may have altered the composition of the underpainting in these areas, though not of course because he had already had an opportunity to witness deterioration in the preceding bay. There is much more green in the preparation of flesh areas than in the preceding bay.

Except for surfaces that have been affected by infiltration of moisture, which has in places even thrown off the intonaco, the fresco is rather well preserved. The large tree, however, has deteriorated greatly; the greens as usual have changed color and fallen away. The olive fruits have proved more resistant.

The three tympana of the church, each in a different patch, differ noticeably in quality, suggesting, therefore, much collaboration. The ornament in patch 11 is well painted, that in 9 grossly, while the figures in 8, set against a gilded field (now mostly lost), are beautiful (Fig. 49*a*). Indeed the liveliest painting in this fresco is not in the figures below, but in the central tympanum and the angels and prophets distributed over the blue, red, and gold façade of the church.

In the painting of this façade a fine fluent style is accompanied by an impressive variety of fresh observations. The simulated statue in the main tympanum is decisively seen from far below (Fig. 49*a*), an application to a figure of an optic principle applied earlier in the cycle to architecture. The low point of sight for the statue is implied by the view of the lower edge of the tunic, and by the appearance of the head of the saint in front of the molding that is actually at a higher level. These figures are superior to the simulated sculpture earlier in the cycle — the winged putti, for instance, in the ciborium in Scene XIII (Fig. 40*c*, p. 117). Similarly, the relief of the eagle in this ciborium is a pale specimen compared with the magnificent eagle at the top of the façade in XXIII (Fig. 49*b*). This powerful predator is approached only by Giovanni Pisano's fiery eagle on the Perugia fountain, but the painter, who no doubt knew Giovanni's relief, studied a live, feathery bird as well.

No less remarkable are the painter's observations of "live" light and shade. To the left of each of the prophets in the pediment is a band of shadow (Fig. 49*b*), and a smaller patch lies to the left of the capital of the pier at the right. These must be considered primordial cast shadows, even though they imply a light coming from the right whereas the main mass of the church (Fig. 49*c*) and the figures below are struck by a light coming from the left. The similar shadows in Scene XVIII also imply a source of light opposite to the one effective for the composition as a whole. Inconsistency within a single space does not, however, diminish the importance of these early observations of shadows, just as it does not lessen the significance of contemporary essays in linear perspective. That the painter has a vivid conception of solid bodies interfering with light is proved not only by the painting of the clerestory of the nave in shade (Fig. 49*c*) but, more strikingly, by the darkness of the statues that stand within brightly-lit canopies (Fig. 49*d*).

49. Scene XXIII, *St. Clare Grieving over the Body of St. Francis at S. Damiano.*
Assisi, S. Francesco.

49a. *Tympanum of church*
   (detail of Scene XXIII).

49b. *Pediment of church*
   (detail of Scene XXIII).
49c. *Clerestory of church*
   (detail of Scene XXIII).
49d. *Pinnacle of church*
   (detail of Scene XXIII).

These precocious analyses of light and shade seem to have established a tradition in the workshops of the church. Some years later a follower of Giotto undertook to paint a bust of Christ on the soffit of the small round arch over the door leading from the Lower Church to the monastery (Fig. 50). The painter seems identical with the author of the allegories in the vaults of the Lower Church; in other words a master of no great endowment. Yet such was the artistic atmosphere in the shops of the church that he was moved, in special circumstances, to create an extraordinary image. This small western door was then, and still is, the only considerable source of light in the very dark Lower Church. In the afternoon, especially, a dazzling beam of light strikes through it into the gloom of the interior. When executing his fresco the painter identified the light on the face of Christ with the actual light, even though this involved shifting the normal and indeed invariable source of the light in paintings from "above" to "below." In a reproduction — the first, so far as we know, of this fresco — "verticality" distorts the effect of a figure actually right overhead, but even in the original the unexpected lighting is as eerie as it is original. The black spots on the cheeks are of course the residue of highlights laid in white lead.

50. Follower of Giotto,
Christ. Assisi,
Lower Church of
S. Francesco.

XXIV

The Canonization

WATER, entering no doubt from the window above, has destroyed almost all of the upper third of this fresco, and much of the rest. In the remaining fragments we recognize the same long bands of heads as in the preceding four frescoes. The scene is equally populous, and the yellow preparatory "wash" drawing in the flesh areas is precisely like that in the preceding bay, and equally evocative and strong (Fig. 51a). Most of the surviving painting in this scene, however, is — like that in the lower part of XXIII — stiff and lifeless (Fig. 51b).

51. Scene XXIV, *The Canonization*. Assisi, S. Francesco.

145

51a. *Friars* (detail of
Scene XXIV).
51b. *Women and Chi*
(detail of Scene x

XXV

Pope Gregory's Vision of the Stigmatized Saint

THIS EPISODE, unlike the ceremonial ones preceding it, scarcely would permit the introduction of many figures. The chief painter, probably the same master responsible (with at least two assistants) for the rest of this bay and the preceding one, has curbed his desire for populous scenes, but he has nevertheless added four figures — the watchers — not mentioned by the *Legenda Maior* of Bonaventura, which was his text. Even the difference of subject does not however conceal some change in the painter's art. The chamber of Gregory IX, actually very large, is made to seem still larger by the simplification of the entire design. Each of the forms, such as the canopy, and each of the figures is comprehended as a separate entity in extended space, and this new clarification is perhaps a consequence of the painter's increasing experience with murals, if our hypothesis about his unfamiliarity with the medium when he began in Scene xx is correct. Perhaps, too, he was influenced by the St. Cecilia Master, who may already have arrived in the church.

This new command and this unprecedented monumentality are evident also in the divisions of the intonaco — large, rational, rectangular. Notable is the union, facilitated by the composition, of the head and body on the same patch in the instance of every figure, even the saint. It may be, however, that we have been unable to detect, in the neck, one of this master's skilfully masked joints. It is interesting that the painter singled out for special treatment the hands and the vial of blood that the saint gives to the Pope. The blood that filled the vial, however, was painted *a secco* and has mostly disappeared.

The aesthetic consequences of decay vary. In this fresco, loss of some of the original color has, it seems to us, given to the interior a sense of spacious atmosphere not imagined by the painter. In the drapery hanging around the room large blue rhomboids containing gold patterns have largely disappeared. The design in the border of this drapery, now gray, was originally gold on a blue ground.

52. Scene xxv, *Pope Gregory's Vision of the Stigmatized Saint*. Assisi, S. Francesco.

XXVI

The Healing of the Man from Ilerda

THE THREE FRESCOES in the last bay are unanimously attributed to the St. Cecilia Master. Their distinctive authorship is reflected in the pattern of divisions of the intonaco. While the figures in each fresco are rather numerous, the number of patches is relatively small and invariable, 7 in XXVI and 8, or at most 9, in XXVII and XXVIII. Though the patches are large, and often contain several figures or numerous forms, a very high proportion of the surface is in fresco. Blue areas painted in azurite are the chief exception to the use of *buon fresco*, and they are not numerous. The divisions are orderly, often rectangular, and like other aspects of the technique of these frescoes, they seem the work of an experienced fresco painter.

In simplicity and rectangularity the divisions in the preceding fresco (xxv) approximate this one. Perhaps the St. Cecilia Master influenced the painter of the preceding two bays, as the latter progressed from XXIII to XXV. But the style of XXV remains readily distinguishable from that of the last bay: the composition, for one thing, is broader and squarer, without the vertical accents of the last bay. The distinctive yellow drawing in XXIII–XXV yields to a predominantly umber drawing in the paintings of the St. Cecilia Master. The St. Cecilia Master employs more terra verde in the flesh areas, and his reds and blues are more dense. But these denser colors are contrasted with transparent ones, such as the exquisite luminous green originally shot with gold in the mantle of the angel nearest the saint.

In keeping with the principle established for the series the mantles of the angels, as supernatural beings, are striated. Their presence — they are not mentioned in the *Legenda Maior* — signifies the miraculous appearance of St. Francis after his death to heal the wounded Spaniard. In the cloak in patch 4 only the gray fresco preparation for blue remains.

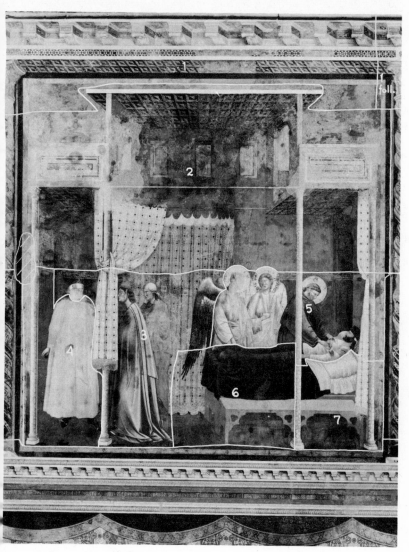

53. Scene XXVI, *The Healing of the Man from Ilerda*. Assisi, S. Francesco.

XXVII

The Confession of the Resuscitated Woman

ONCE AGAIN the painter executed the fresco with great despatch, moving regularly and with great assurance down the wall. And again the proportion of true fresco is large, although the blue areas painted *a secco* and now disintegrated are more numerous than in XXVI. They include the dress of the woman at the left in 6, the dress of the woman at the right in 6 and 7, and the bedcover in 8. The mantle of the stout priest in 5, which has partly disappeared, was painted in malachite or a similar green.

54. Scene XXVII, *The Confession of the Resuscitated Woman*. Assisi, S. Francesco.

XXVIII

St. Francis Liberates the Repentant Heretic

AS IN XXVI AND XXVII the boundaries of the large patches coincide neatly with boundaries of the forms represented. Only the requirement of a figure at a lower level, the kneeling bishop, disturbs the regular shapes of the patches. 3 seems to us abnormally large even for this highly accomplished fresco painter, especially because it contains the saint flying back to heaven after the miracle, and a many-figured frieze winding around the column *alla Traiana* (Fig. 55a). Furthermore, the strange building at the left contains a row of niches filled with figures holding scrolls, all quickly and beautifully painted in a rich green fresco. Whether or not this patch was divided at the center is difficult to discover because of damage.

Most of the painting is true fresco. The cope of the ecclesiastic with upraised hands, however, was finished with azurite. A metallic paint was laid *a secco* on all the metal objects at the right: the sword, the armor of the soldiers, and the shackles, miraculously opened by St. Francis and still leaving marks on the legs of the heretic who brandishes them before his episcopal imprisoner. In front of the shield the hand of the soldier, probably sheathed with metal, was painted *a secco* while the two hands of the ex-heretic are in fresco.

55. Scene XXVIII, *St. Francis Liberates the Repentant Heretic*. Assisi, S. Francesco.

55a. Spiral frieze (detail of Scene XXVIII).

CHAPTER 5

Observations on the Arena Chapel

and Santa Croce

56. Giotto, frescoes (detail). Padua, Arena Chapel.

THOUGH much would surely be gained by an attempt to place the *Legend* in the context of early Trecento mural procedures, a comprehensive study of this sort is beyond the scope of the present book. More time than was available to us would be required for an exploration of the technique and the intonaco pattern of major monuments of the time, and for each we would have needed a movable scaffold of adequate height. We are however unwilling to leave the *Legend* and the preceding murals in the Upper Church isolated except for scattered comments about related aspects of other paintings. We therefore present at this point brief observations, first on the frescoes in the Arena Chapel, which among surviving cycles are chronologically closest to the *Legend*. We shall conclude with a few words on the two later cycles by Giotto in Santa Croce.

In the Arena Chapel we have examined only the frescoes on the chancel arch and those adjacent to it on the nave walls (see Diagram K). This group offers specimens, however, of the main stages in the painting of the chapel because there are two scenes from each tier of frescoes, and only the entrance wall is not represented (Fig. 56). Study of the intonaco has enabled us to give a definitive answer to a question that has been debated for many years.

Throughout this century historians have commented on the similarities between the uppermost tier of frescoes representing episodes from the life of the Virgin and the lowest tier representing Vices and Virtues. In 1911 Axel Romdahl interpreted these similarities as the result of the execution of the two tiers in immediate chronological succession. The life of the Virgin was, he judged, an addition

unforeseen at the outset and painted after the Vices and Virtues.[1]
This thesis was rejected in the great monograph by Rintelen published in the following year,[2] and it has not been generally accepted
since then. From time to time, however, it has been revived, by
Vitzthum for instance in 1929[3] and by Baumgart at great length in
1937.[4] This view is incorrect. The overlapping of the patches of
intonaco prove beyond any question that on both nave walls as well
as on the triumphal arch Giotto worked in the normal and practical
sequence, from above down (see Diagram K).[5]

In contrast with the greater part of the *Legend* in Assisi white
lead is not employed in the frescoes in the Arena Chapel. The lack
of it is one reason for the enduring transparency of the colors and
their relatively good preservation, which matches the breathtaking
brilliance of the painting. Even in the *Expulsion of Joachim from
the Temple* (Fig. 57), one of the very first scenes to be undertaken and thus closest to the *Legend* in the commonly held sequence
of Giotto's work,[6] there is no white lead whatever (Fig. 57a). Furthermore the torso and the feet of each of the two standing figures
visible in full length are united in one patch. Such an organic unity
appears to be normal though not invariable in the Chapel, whereas
it is abnormal, as we have seen, in the frescoes in the *Legend* in
Assisi (II–XIII) that are considered the best representatives of Giotto's art.

One aspect of the procedure in this early fresco in Padua is entirely unprecedented in the cycle in Assisi. Changes in any of the
scenes of the *Legend* after the intonaco was spread are very exceptional. In the first two frescoes in Assisi, to be sure, the garments of
two figures (one by the St. Cecilia Master) were given a final form
slightly different from that foreseen when the intonaco was spread.
To our knowledge no head was changed correspondingly in any of
the twenty-eight frescoes. But in the *Expulsion of Joachim* the head
of the young man who is blessed by the priest was painted partly on
patch 2 and partly on 4 (Fig. 57b). Such a division could not have
been planned, because of the difficulty of an exact match of the colors, and an intonaco joint in the area of a face is always avoided. At
some moment after 2 was laid, Giotto decided to lower the upper

57. Giotto, *Expulsion of Joachim from the Temple*. Padua, Arena Chapel.

edge of the wall of the sanctuary as well as shift its angle, while disclosing more of the man's head. The part of the face that was added was left, however, in greenish-gray, either because of an oversight or a wish to suggest shade.

It is fascinating to observe that this is only the last of three changes Giotto made at this place. On patch 2 there are two red earth lines showing the rim of the sanctuary at levels above the joint. The precise reasons for these changes of mind are not entirely clear. It is conceivable that at one moment the painter decided to show there the upper surface of the wall, which is indeed visible behind the altar and the priest, but there are no clear signs of such an intention along the section of wall below the priest. Whether Giotto was more interested in shifting the angle of the wall or in exposing a larger

57a. Joachim and the High Priest (detail of Fig. 57).

portion of the head cannot definitely be said, but the addition of the mouth and jaw to this quiet, receptive face heightens the contrast with the rejected Joachim so much that we may safely assume Giotto had this in mind when altering the design.

Other beholders of this sublime painting may have sometimes wondered, as we did, whether the astonishing and highly expressive void into which old Joachim is pushed was always entirely lacking in forms. It was.

The fresco opposite the *Expulsion of Joachim*, the *Virgin Returning from the Temple*, is no less exalted, but it is damaged by water,

57b. Head of a youth (detail of Fig. 57).

especially at the right, and disturbed by an unnecessary grill that will, we hope, soon be removed (Fig. 58). Here again the bodies and the feet are together on the intonaco, noteworthy especially where the legs and feet are exposed below the garments. In order to keep the Virgin's mantle and train together patch 8 dips way out to the left.

Most interesting of all are alterations of the design made during the course of painting. Giotto became dissatisfied, as he worked, with the heavy cylindrical mass of the figure in front of the Virgin (Figs. 58a and 58b). He quickly modified it by two superficial addi-

58. Giotto, *Virgin Returning from the Temple*. Padua, Arena Chapel.

58a. *The Virgin and companions*
(detail of Fig. 58).

58b. *A mantle repainted by Giotto*
(detail of Fig. 58).

59. Giotto, *Nativity*. Padua, Arena Chapel.

tions. He raised the skirt a little by running over its lower border a strip the color of the ground on which the figures stand. He reduced the monolithic massiveness of the mantle by painting a thin red line over it from the lower left to the right above the level of the knees. By this single genial stroke the garment is transformed from a mantle into a mantle over a tunic. The garb of the figure thus resembles the Virgin's, and the ascending movement of the edge of her mantle is echoed by the pseudo-mantle alongside. The changes beyond any doubt reveal the mind, and probably the touch, of the master himself.

The *Nativity* too was altered during the course of the painting (Fig. 59). The upper outline of the Virgin originally coincided with the joint between patches 3 and 5. The suture would normally follow the contour of the figure, and a red preparatory line along the

60l. Giotto, *Annunciation* (left). Padua, Arena Chapel.

6or. Giotto, *Annunciation* (right). Padua, Arena Chapel.

61. Giotto, *Visitation*. Padua, Arena Chapel.

upper edge of 5 proves that, when the intonaco was laid, the painter still intended the figure to extend to that level. All these scenes, as well as the *Annunciation* (Figs. 6ol and 6or) and the *Visitation* (Fig. 61), were painted mostly in *buon fresco*. In the *Nativity*, however, some of the beautiful clear blue has come off the mantle of the Virgin and all of it from Joseph's tunic. In the *Return of the Virgin* diagonal stripes applied *a secco* have largely peeled off the tunic of

62. Giotto, *Expulsion of the Tradesmen from the Temple*. Padua, Arena Chapel.

the violinist, and the last man in this scene has lost the blue of his dress as well as his trumpet (Fig. 58, p. 164). For the same reason the walls of the room of the *Last Supper* (Fig. 67, p. 179), now bare, have lost all their ornament.

Losses in the *Expulsion of the Tradesmen from the Temple* have more seriously affected the reading of the design (Fig. 62). The boxes and crates in the foreground, now all in various stages of disintegration, originally were prominent in the composition and the narrative. The door of the cage held by the agitated young vendor nearest Christ has fallen open, and the birds have escaped through it, vanishing presumably in the direction of the fleeing goats. The crate in front of the man in 12, not yet disturbed, contains five pigeons; they were painted *a secco* and are invisible from the floor of the

62a. Giotto, *Skirt of Christ* (detail of Fig. 62).

Chapel today. The framework of the upturned table in front of Christ has disintegrated also, especially those parts painted *a secco* over his mantle. The loss of part of this form has weakened the horizontal movement along the ground, originally powerful as it extended from the animals at the left (actually also facing to the left) through the market boxes to the scampering animals at the right. The figure of Christ, which now interposes a massive uninterrupted vertical at the center of the design, was originally contained in a shallow space between two wooden structures, the farther one higher than the nearer.

This relationship between the two containing forms was not finally decided without some deliberation. In fact, at this point we again get an insight into Giotto's procedures, comparable to the one in the *Expulsion of Joachim* discussed above. The blue applied in tempera to Christ's mantle has mostly fallen away, exposing the red fresco preparation. On this surface the painter has sketched some lines for a structure that corresponds with neither of those actually painted (Fig. 62*a*). The lines begin at the level of the feet of the triangular crate behind Christ, but they rise higher than it does. A change of this sort might be interpreted as the consequence of the lack of a full-scale drawing on the *arriccio*, but it involves a secondary, nonfigural form, and it would be rash to draw inferences from one or two instances.

It was not only during the course of the work that Giotto changed his mind at several places in this fresco. Even after part of the paint was dry, or the entire scene was completed, he altered forms or in-

63. Byzantine, twelfth century, *Christ Cleansing the Temple*. Monreale, Cathedral.

troduced new ones. He had adopted for the *Expulsion* the main groups of the Byzantine composition of this scene (Fig. 63): the apostles behind Christ, the fleeing tradesmen, the troubled, plotting Pharisees at the right, and in the background the temple, which may owe its strange round lunettes above and its two prancing horses between two lions to S. Marco in Venice.[7] Giotto departed, however, from the normal iconography of the event in one very interesting respect. Looking at his fresco one would conclude that the temple was contaminated only by the purveyors of sacrificial birds and animals. The paraphernalia of another kind of business disrupted by Christ, the coin scales knocked over, the careening table spilling money in all directions, and the large purses carried off by anxious owners,[8] as in the mosaic in Monreale (Fig. 63), all are lacking.

The Gospels as well as most large representations emphasized the overthrow of the tables of the money changers. It is not surprising that the scene in the Arena Chapel as elsewhere should often be entitled the *Expulsion of the Money Changers from the Temple*,[9] but the only object that seems to allude to this occupation is the table lying quietly, face-downward, in front of Christ. At best therefore Giotto pays only lip service to tradition. It would be wrong of course to suppose that the calling largely suppressed in the scene was unknown to Giotto and his patron. Enrico Scrovegni's father, Reginaldo, was a notorious money lender who was confined by Dante to the seventh circle of Hell for the crime of usury. Money changing was not ecclesiastically as sensitive an occupation as money lending, but the two were in actual practice commonly combined.

In connection with this diminution of references to money in the *Cleansing* it is interesting to recall other representations of it in the Arena Chapel. The fact that people overly attached to money are bound to sacks of it in the *Last Judgment* might seem to reflect a different attitude. *Caritas*, furthermore, tramples moneybags underfoot. The vice opposed to this virtue however is not the usual Avarice, but Envy (Fig. 64). Envy does, it is true, clutch a bag presumably of coins, but the emphasis is shifted from a lust for money to the more comprehensive covetousness of *Invidia*, and in this shift Giotto went further than one of the great representatives of early capitalism, Giovanni Villani, who still included avarice among the capital sins, although he traced its origin to envy.[10] Giotto's revision of the vice opposed to *Caritas* is related to the fact that no money changers are explicitly expelled from the temple. For subtle reasons about which we can only rather uncertainly speculate, it was decided to include this very rare scene [11] but at the same time to omit major personages from the cast of characters. It is a rather bold attempt to revise the representational tradition, not to mention the Gospels.

One other aspect of the story is novel. At the left a young apostle is sheltering a child in his mantle, lowering his head so that his face, astonishingly, is in shade. The child, terrified by the anger of the Lord, "molto terribile nella faccia," as Chapter 42 of the *Meditazioni sulla vita di Gesù Cristo* describes him, was the only figure moving away from Christ toward the left when the painting was completed. The bullocks strengthened this movement, but Giotto judged it was not properly mediated; he felt that the passage toward the left from the figure of Christ (lunging toward the right) to the columnar figure of St. Peter and the child near the frame was abrupt and

64. Giotto, *Invidia*.
Padua, Arena Chapel.

65. Giotto, *Child with dove* (detail of Fig. 62, p. 169).

insufficiently rhythmical. He decided, partly at least for this reason, to introduce a mediator, like the famous one between Christ and Lazarus in the *Raising*. In this instance it was to be, largely for lack of space, a child.

Giotto cut out a piece of intonaco from the yellow mantle of St. Peter, laid a fresh patch, and on it painted in fresco the upper part of a child (Figs. 62, 65). Evidently his preference for *buon fresco* was strong, but the fresh patch proved in the end not large enough and the figure was completed in a summary way by red and blue lines painted *a secco* right over Peter's yellow mantle.

Giotto's greatness as an artist and his close relationship to the medieval tradition have not induced us to think of him as a painter with problems and alternatives.[12] The very perfection of the Arena frescoes seems to still thought about the process of creation, and historians incline to conceive of him as Vasari conceived of Fra Angelico, unwilling to retouch any of his works and preferring to leave them as they had first come out, in the belief that this was the will of God.[13] But a close study of just a few frescoes proves that for Giotto, as for later artists, creation was a process of sustained searching, of choice and rejection, and, like many great writers, he was still wont to make changes in galley and even page proof.

Other trials and changes are visible in the *Expulsion*. A curved red line just to the right of Christ's profile suggests that at one moment the painter thought the head would be placed more to the right and given thus a still more aggressive thrust. The head of the apostle who shields the child was drawn about six inches to the right of its present position; part of the outline may be seen on the chest of St. Peter where the blue has now fallen away. After the halo of the middle apostle of the three at the left was completed its width was doubled.

The little figure added to the composition after the left part, at least, had been completed is not of course simply a new link in a chain of movement but a new actor in a drama. The presence of children is unprecedented in the representation of the cleansing of the temple, but they play a role in other scenes in the Arena Chapel, such as the *Entry into Jerusalem* and the *Raising of Lazarus*. They "invade" other subjects at the time, such as the *Way to Calvary*, freely venting feelings shared but not so overtly expressed by adults.[14] In Italian art beginning in the late thirteenth century *amor proximi* is exemplified by a woman tending not a beggar but a child, and miracles of rescued or revived children are favorite subjects of Trecento art.

Perhaps the form taken by Giotto's afterthought was suggested by the man holding birds who occasionally appears among the

66. Giotto, *Pact of Judas*. Padua, Arena Chapel.

evicted tradesmen in medieval representations of the Purging.[15] On
the other hand there is warrant in the text of Matthew (21:15) for
the introduction of children at the time of the expulsion: "But when
the chief priests and the scribes saw the wonderful things that he
did, and the children that were crying in the temple and saying,
Hosanna to the son of David; they were moved with indigna-
tion. . . . " Giotto's children, however, far from hailing Christ, flee
from his angry aggression. They act, in other words, at the common
human rather than the religious or symbolic level.

176

66a. Giotto, *Judas, the devil, and a priest* (detail of Fig. 66).

Perhaps another extraordinary aspect of the child added on the new patch is to be understood in this sense only. He is clutching a dove, presumably one of those that escaped from the opened cages rather than one bought before the arrival of Christ. But the closeness of the child to St. Peter, from whose mantle he was actually created, and his identification with the group of apostles, inevitably suggests an association with the Holy Ghost, which inspired the apostles at Pentecost. The sacrificial bird seems to be rescued and transformed by the work of Christ, but it is probably too much to suggest that in this remarkable and wholly unprecedented representation there is latent an idea of Christian progress from the Old Testament to the New.

It is an interesting fact that, though the traditional figure clutching his moneybag is not visible in the *Expulsion*, a very similar man appears in the next scene, at the right on the adjacent triumphal arch (Fig. 66). One almost has the impression that Judas has escaped from the temple to treat, in the next episode, with the priests; and continuity is, in another regard, explicitly indicated by the three priests, who are identical with the three plotting apprehensively in the preceding scene. Of course, Judas has gotten his money not from financial affairs but from a traitorous conspiracy. It is his part in the evil betrayal that is condemned in this remarkably sinister scene.

Because of its peculiar shape and black color the present halo of Judas (Fig. 66a) has given rise to speculation. There are, however, unmistakable traces of the lower half of the disk on patch 3; the material has simply adhered better on one patch than another, a common phenomenon attributable in this instance perhaps to remaining dampness in the intonaco of 3 when the halo was applied *a secco*. Not only Judas but all the disciples wear similar haloes in the two subsequent scenes in the story, the *Last Supper* (Fig. 67) and the *Washing of the Feet*, both painted on the opposite wall.[16]

Analysis in a laboratory of a minute specimen of the substance in these darkened haloes proves it to have been composed of lead, copper, silver, and a little gold; a false gold, in other words, that has oxidized.[17] Cennino Cennini, in Chapter 101, writes of an imitation-gold halo made of gilded tin, but he does not describe the material used in the Arena Chapel.

Though the haloes of Judas and the other apostles in these scenes are composed of the same metal a distinction is preserved between them: the haloes of the apostles have rays, while his alone in all three scenes is perfectly smooth. In the *Last Supper* and the *Washing of the Feet* there are in fact three kinds of haloes: 1) gold and in relief for Christ; 2) without relief, simulated gold, with rays, for the apostles; 3) the same as 2, but without rays, for Judas. Haloes are varied throughout the cycle in accordance with different purposes but with a high degree of consistency, as far as we could judge from the floor. A principle is established in what probably was the first surface painted by Giotto in the chapel, the angels high on the chancel arch. Here all the haloes are in relief except those of the

67. Giotto, *Last Supper*. Padua, Arena Chapel.

two angels at each side that are both close to the enframing arch and, what is decisive, deepest in space. A halo without relief is used similarly for the angel deepest in space and closest to the frame in the *Baptism* and for the one in a corresponding position on the empty tomb. The same spatial considerations seem to have governed the flat haloes of the apostles in the *Raising of Lazarus* and in the *Pentecost* (Fig. 68), where the apostles in the front row have haloes in relief, while those deeper in space have not. Iconographic factors seem more important in the choice of flat haloes for the centurion in the *Crucifixion*, for the figures immediately to the left and right of Lazarus, and the apostle at table in the *Marriage at Cana*.

The only mural paintings after those in the Arena Chapel that were carried out under the supervision, at least, of Giotto are much

68. Giotto and assistants, *Pentecost*. Padua, Arena Chapel.

later in date and therefore less relevant to our central subject, the *Legend* in Assisi. The intonaco pattern in the one scene in the Bardi Chapel that we were able to map shows, despite the regrettable dammage, the characteristic mosaic of fresco (Fig. 69). Several distinctive painters carried out the commission in this chapel, but they all tended to relegate more of the work to a tempera technique than Giotto had done at Padua. Thus the head and hands of St. Francis in the *Appearance at Arles* were painted entirely in fresco, but his habit was only prepared in this technique and completed on a dry, or nearly dry, wall (Fig. 70). The extent of the completion *a secco* may account for the large size of patch x in the scene of the *Death* (Fig. 69). Some changes on the intonaco are visible, but fewer than in the Arena Chapel. In the scene of the saint denying his father, the

69. Giotto and assistants, *Death of St. Francis*. Florence, S. Croce, Bardi Chapel.

70. Assistant of Giotto, *St. Francis*. Florence, S. Croce, Bardi Chapel.

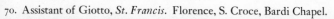

71. Giotto and assistants, *Heads and palace* (detail of *St. Francis Renouncing His Wealth*). Florence, S. Croce, Bardi Chapel.

molding over the heads of the figures was given a steeper decline on both sides of the building (Fig. 71). And the position finally assumed by the head and hand of the friar in the *Death* who looks up at the ascending saint differs slightly from the outlines still clearly visible alongside. Nowhere are there any traces of sinopia drawings on the *arriccio*.

In the Peruzzi Chapel Giotto and his assistants returned, as we have said, to secco painting (Fig. 72). Secco painting, but not pure secco, because just as fresco painting is normally combined with a certain amount of secco, so secco often includes some fresco — as in the "fresco secco" technique to which we have referred above (p. 7). Colors such as the pink on the tower behind the violinist in *Herod's Feast* that were spread while part of the plaster in the huge patches was still damp have been fixed in the process of carbonation.[18] The intonaco in the Peruzzi Chapel was laid in the large rec-

72. Giotto and assistants, *Ascension of St. John the Evangelist*. Florence, S. Croce, Peruzzi Chapel.

tangles of the *pontata*, two patches to a scene, with the joint between them falling near the neck and shoulders of the majority of the figures. Since each scene, from inner border to inner border, measures about 8½ feet high the *pontate* were about 4¼ feet high. The supporting beams of the scaffold were fixed in the wall, and the places into which they fitted were plastered separately. Either the removal of the beams or the plastering of these squares was deferred until the *pontate* had been spread and had dried. The levels of the scaffold were so close that a man could not stand up, much less work comfortably, on one platform if the boards above were left in place.

In technique the Peruzzi Chapel is further removed than the Bardi Chapel from the cycle at Padua. This greater difference might suggest that the Peruzzi Chapel was painted later than the Bardi. However the need for great speed or other considerations at which we can only guess might have been responsible for the readoption of a technique that heretofore historians, guided by Cennino, believed had been decisively outmoded by Giotto. As Anatole France reminds us: "... L'embarras de l'historien s'accroît avec l'abondance des documents." (*L'île des pingouins.*)

NOTES

1. "Stil und Chronologie der Arenafresken Giottos," *Jahrbuch der preussischen Kunstsammlungen*, XXXII, 1911, pp. 3–18.

2. *Giotto und die Giotto-Apokryphen*, Munich, 1912, p. 15, note 29.

3. "Zu Giottos *Navicella*," in *Festschrift Paul Schubring*, Leipzig, 1929, pp. 150 ff.

4. F. Baumgart, "Die Fresken Giottos in Padua," *Zeitschrift für Kunstgeschichte*, VI, 1937, pp. 1 ff.

5. Some historians have proposed also a chronological order of work within each tier. Thus Baumgart (*op. cit.*) concluded that the lowest row on the left hand side (facing the choir) was painted from the entrance wall to the triumphal arch, that is, from the *Way to Calvary* to the *Pentecost*, whereas the opposite wall was painted in the opposite direction, from the *Last Supper* to the *Mockery*. A test of the intonaco on the left hand wall near the triumphal arch shows that there at least Giotto and his assistants painted the vertical ornamental bands between the scenes before the adjacent scenes themselves, so that it is impossible to discover the sequence of the scenes themselves (or the bands).

Almost all scholars have recognized that Giotto employed assistants in the Arena Chapel, especially for the execution of the decorative bands but also for the scenes. It has not however been pointed out, as far as we know, that the simulated chapel on the right side of the chancel arch is inferior to that on the left, and probably a copy of it.

6. This inclusion of the *Legend* in Giotto's early oeuvre is, however, contested by (among a few others) Millard Meiss. See his *Giotto and Assisi*, New York, 1960.

7. For the usual Byzantine composition see O. Demus, *The Mosaics of Norman Sicily*, London, 1949, p. 279. See also the fresco at Curtea de Arges [O. Tafrali, *Monuments byzantins de Curtea de Arges*, Paris, 1913, pl. XLIX(2)]; Paris, Bibl. Nat. gr. 74 fol. 170v. (Paris, Bibl. Nat., *Ms. gr. 74 ... Evangiles avec peintures du XIe siècle*, Paris, 1908, pl. 148(1). Especially relevant is the twelfth-century painting in Schwarzrheindorf (E. Aus'm Weerth, *Wandmalereien des Christlichen Mittelalters in den Rheinlanden*, Leipzig, 1880, pl. XXVI, figs. 1–3).

8. For example, the relief on the

façade of St. Gilles (R. Hamann, *St. Gilles*, Berlin, 1955, pls. 56, 57).

See also the panel in Ghiberti's North Door (R. Krautheimer, *Lorenzo Ghiberti*, Princeton, 1956, pl. 34).

9. See for instance Van Marle, *op. cit.*, III, p. 84 and VI (iconographic index), p. 40.

10. This was pointed out by Meiss, *Painting in Florence and Siena after the Black Death*, p. 50, note 147.

11. We cannot think of another example in Trecento painting. Nor does Van Marle, *loc. cit.*, cite one.

12. Borsook (*op. cit.*, p. 130) observed that in the *Last Judgment* the blue azurite mantle of Christ was lowered somewhat over the red tunic, and that a cap or two were added in the crowd of the Blessed.

13. *Vite*, ed. Milanesi, Florence, 1906, II, p. 520. "Aveva per costume non ritoccare nè racconciare mai alcuna sua dipintura, ma lasciarle sempre in quel modo che erano venute la prima volta, per credere (secondo ch'egli diceva) che così fusse la volontà di Dio."

14. On the role of children in early fourteenth-century art see Meiss, *op. cit.*, p. 61. For an instance of children in the Way to Calvary see Simone Martini's panel in the Louvre (Van Marle, *op. cit.*, II, fig. 163).

15. F. X. Kraus, *Codex Egberti*, Freiburg i/B, 1884, pl. XXXII. Also a late Byzantine psalter at Mount Athos, Pantokrater 61, fol. 87.

16. The haloes of the two angels behind the cross in the *Last Judgment* are similar.

17. For the analysis of the metal in the haloes we are indebted to the Conservation Center of the Institute of Fine Arts of New York University, particularly to Lawrence Majewski, Research Associate of the Center, and Dr. Edward V. Sayre, Consulting Fellow.

18. Over the window of the chapel there is a roundel containing a Lamb on an altar, all executed in *buon fresco*, but perhaps painted somewhat later than the large frescoes. Possibly it replaces a roundel painted in this area originally.

SELECTIVE LIST OF TECHNICAL STUDIES

L. B. Alberti's Kleinere Kunsttheoretische Schriften, ed. by H. Janitschek, Vienna, 1877.

Augusti, S., "La tecnica dell' antica pittura parietale pompeiana," in *Pompeiana, Raccolta di studi per il secondo centenario degli scavi di Pompei,* Naples, 1950, pp. 313–54.

Berger, E., *Quellen und Technik der Fresko-, Oele-, und Tempera-Malerei des Mittelalters,* 2nd ed., Munich, 1912.

Borsook, E., *The Mural Painters of Tuscany,* London, 1960.

Cennino Cennini, *Il libro dell' arte,* ed. by D. V. Thompson, Jr., New Haven, 1933.

Gettens, R. J., and Stout, G. L., "A Monument of Byzantine Wall Painting —the Method of Construction," in *Studies in Conservation,* III, 1958, 107–18.

Klinkert, W., "Bemerkungen zur Technik der Pompejanischen Wanddekoration," in L. Curtius, *Die Wandmalerei Pompejis,* Hildesheim, 1960, pp. 435–72.

Kitzinger, E., *The Mosaics of Monreale,* Palermo, 1960, pp. 64–68.

Lehmann, P. W., *Roman Wall Paintings from Boscoreale in the Metropolitan Museum of Art,* Cambridge (Mass.), 1953, p. 164.

Oertel, R., "Wandmalerei und Zeichnung in Italien," in *Mitteilungen des Kunsthistorischen Instituts in Florenz,* 1940, v, pp. 217–314.

Pliny, *Natural History* (Loeb Library), London, 1952, IX, Book XXXV.

Procacci, U., *Sinopie e Affreschi,* Florence, 1960 (accessible only after this text went to the press).

Procacci, U., *La tecnica degli antichi affreschi e il loro distacco e restauro,* Florence, 1958.

Swindler, M. H., *Ancient Painting,* New Haven, 1929, pp. 417–27.

Theophilus presbyter, *Schedula diversarum artium,* ed. by A. Ilg, Vienna, 1874.

Toesca, P., *Gli affreschi della Vita di San Francesco nella Chiesa Superiore del Santuario di Assisi, Artis Monumenta Photographice Edita,* Florence, 1946, III, 13–18.

Vasari, *Le Vite,* ed. Milanesi, Florence, 1906, I, 181–82, 558.

Vitruvius on Architecture (Loeb Library), London, 1934, II, Book VII, Chapters 3–5.

GLOSSARY

(Several of these words or phrases have been used in English for some time, and are accepted by Webster. They appear in the present text in roman. All these terms are defined more fully and more precisely in Chapter 1.)

Arriccio	The coarser, thicker layer of plaster below the intonaco.
Buon fresco	Painting, mostly with a water vehicle, on wet lime plaster.
Cartoon	A full-scale drawing of a part or the whole of a painting, the lines of which are transferred to the surface on which the painting is to be made.
Fresco secco	Painting with a vehicle of lime water on plaster which, though previously dried, is moistened when the colors are applied.
Giallorino	A yellow color used especially for drawing on intonaco.
Giornate	Patches of intonaco, each representing what the frescoist intended to paint in a day's work.
Intonaco	The uppermost, thin layer of plaster to which the colors are applied. The texture of the intonaco is fine.
Pontate	Large rectangles of intonaco characteristic of secco painting.
Secco	Painting on dry plaster.
Sinopia	Red earth preparatory drawing on the *arriccio*.
Spolvero	A process of transferring the lines of a cartoon to the intonaco by dusting pigment through perforations in them. The word may refer also to the cartoon so used.
Terra verde	Green earth color used especially for shading.
Verdaccio	A mixture of ocher, black, lime white, and cinnabar used for drawing on intonaco.

73. Pannini, detail of S. Paolo f.l.m. showing scenes (now destroyed) of the life of St. Paul by Cavallini. London, Leonard Koetser Gallery.

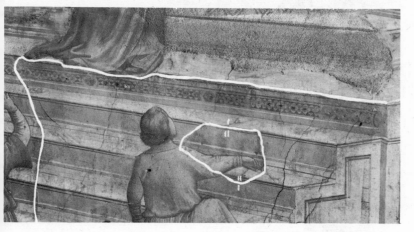

74. Taddeo Gaddi, detail of Fig. 8, p. 23, showing a change in the arm of a youth.

75. Pistoiese Master, fresco, *Presentation of the Virgin*. Pistoia, S. Domenico.

76. Pistoiese Master, sinopia for
Presentation of the Virgin.
Pistoia, S. Domenico.

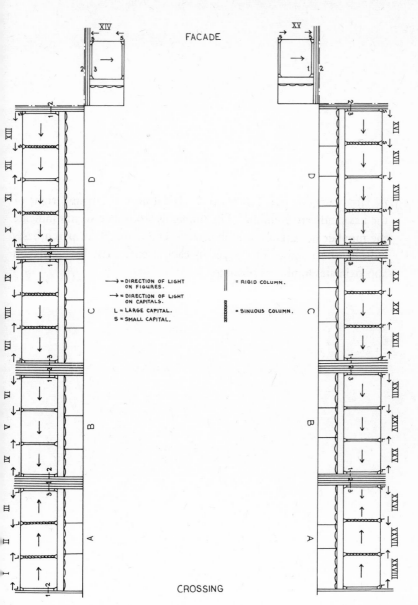

FACADE

= DIRECTION OF LIGHT
ON FIGURES.

→ = DIRECTION OF LIGHT
ON CAPITALS.

L = LARGE CAPITAL.

S = SMALL CAPITAL.

|| = RIGID COLUMN.

= SINUOUS COLUMN.

CROSSING

Diagram A. Plan of frescoes, Scenes I–XXVIII of the life of St. Francis,
in the Upper Church at Assisi.

IN THE DIAGRAMS that follow, the vertical lines at left and right of the bays indicate columns. The numerals below the scenes indicate the number of patches in each scene. The numerals in parentheses indicate the number of figures in each scene; sometimes only an approximate number is possible.

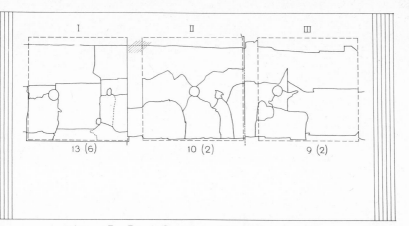

Diagram B. Bay A, Scenes I–III, Upper Church, Assisi.

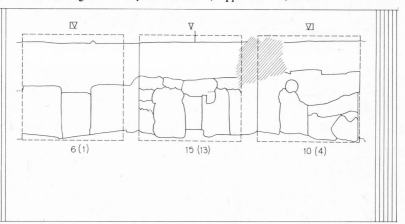

Diagram C. Bay B, Scenes IV–VI, Upper Church, Assisi.

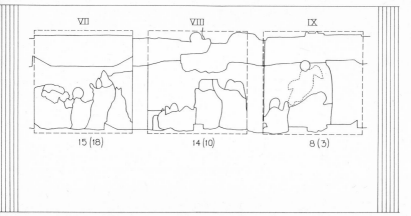

Diagram D. Bay C, Scenes VII–IX, Upper Church, Assisi.

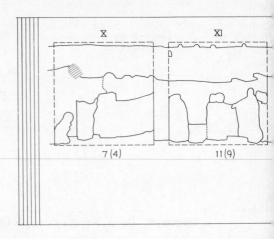

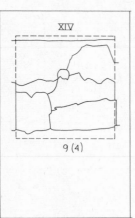

Diagram F.   Facade, Scenes XIV–X

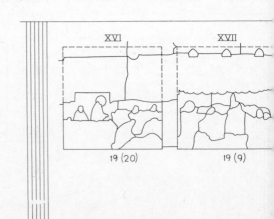

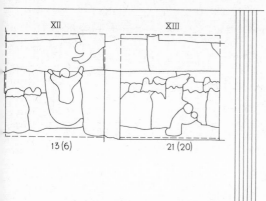

Diagram E.
Bay D, Scenes x–xiii,
Upper Church, Assisi.

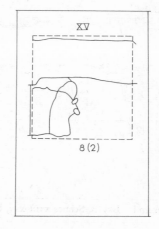

Upper Church, Assisi.

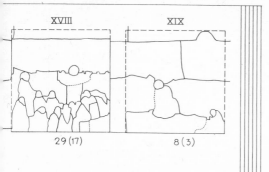

Diagram G.
Bay D, Scenes xvi–xix,
Upper Church, Assisi.

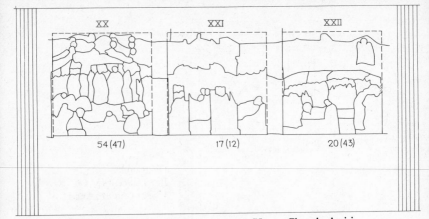

Diagram H. Bay C, Scenes xx–xxii, Upper Church, Assisi.

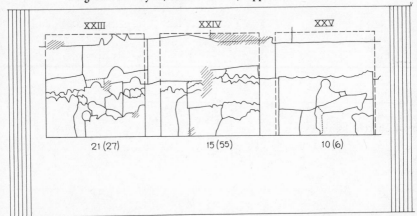

Diagram I. Bay B, Scenes xxiii–xxv, Upper Church, Assisi.

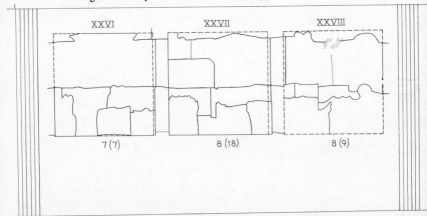

Diagram J. Bay A, Scenes xxvi–xxviii, Upper Church, Assisi.

Diagram K.   Plan of chancel arch, Arena Chapel, Padua.

APPENDIX OF 1964

ADDITIONAL OBSERVATIONS ON
ITALIAN MURAL TECHNIQUE

Inasmuch as the study of mural technique is still in its early stages, it is not surprising that observations recorded only three years ago can be significantly extended.[1] The earlier formulations are in every case the point of departure for the new observations, and it is for this reason that we have preferred to present them to other students now rather than to wait several years for the accumulation of more evidence. Only the participation of numerous explorers will give us a comprehensive view of the development of mural technique from antiquity through the Renaissance. Of course even then the advancement of knowledge is partly dependent upon random events, the accidents of the deterioration of existing cycles and the campaigns for their restoration. As in certain branches of clinical medicine, progress is bound up with the appearance of patients. More rapid forward movement can be accomplished only by the commitment over a period of years of two or three qualified persons, including of course a chemist. It is clearly time to establish a team for the study of the history of mural technique.

In 1962 we attempted to contribute to the hypothesis of a derivation of late mediaeval and Renaissance mural technique from ancient Roman painting (pp. 5–8). While we were unable to demonstrate a continuity —the close study of mediaeval practice still needs to be undertaken— we pointed to the coincidence of the use of fresco in ancient Rome and in the period beginning with the late thirteenth century. The use of fresco—a technique of painting on a freshly spread intonaco that takes advantage of the carbonation of the lime for the incorporation of the pigments in the solid mass of the plaster—has so often been denied to Roman antiquity [2] that we believe it worth while to add to the evidence for its use in the Villa dei Misteri and elsewhere that we presented in 1962. The condition of one unfinished wall in Pompeii is relevant; charred surfaces and objects suggest that the work was abandoned when Vesuvius erupted (Fig. 77). A large patch of intonaco on the upper part of the wall ends irregularly, and at the left it has been cut back to the surface upon which the painter had worked. The marks of the chisel used for this purpose are clearly visible. Evidently the painter wished to carry out part at least of his work on damp intonaco; otherwise the intonaco would have been spread in large patches over the entire wall before the painting was begun. Before or while painting the artist defined the lower limit of his zone by inscribing a straight line. He allowed the strokes of his brush to end irregularly below this line, knowing that the intonaco would be cut back to it. Equally in-

77. Unfinished Roman mural. Pompeii.

78. Roman, *Elephant*. Pompeii, Casa Omerica, Sala degli Elefanti.

79. Giotto, *Expulsion of Joachim* (detail). Padua, Arena Chapel.
Polished *secco su fresco*.

80. Piero della Francesca, *Death of Adam* (detail). Arezzo, S. Francesco,
(photo: Anderson)

81. Piero della Francesca, *Rout of Maxentius* (detail). Arezzo, S. Francesco.
(photo: Soprintendenza Firenze)

structive is the present condition of the painted surface in the Sala degli
Elefanti of the Casa Omerica (Fig. 78).[3] The head and the upper part
of the body of the elephant have undergone changes different from
those of the lower part. The boundary between the two zones forms
a long, slightly curved line that corresponds to a joint in the intonaco. The difference in the surfaces today on the opposite sides of
this boundary are the consequence of a difference in the quality of
the intonaco and/or the paint.

The advocates of the techniques of fresco and secco in Roman antiquity have tended to assume polar positions on the content of the
vehicle of the paint as well as on the condition of the intonaco. Those
who maintain that fresco was employed usually claim or at least imply
that the vehicle was water, while secco of course requires a vehicle
containing a binding medium, whether egg, wax, or some other organic
substance. There are physical signs in Roman murals, however, that
point to the presence of an organic material within the paint that was
applied to the intonaco while it was still damp. From the time of
Vitruvius on it has often been remarked that wax was spread on the
surface of the paintings for the purpose of polishing, but we refer now
to the inclusion of an organic substance in the vehicle of paint to be
used on wet plaster. In many monochromatic surfaces no brushstrokes
are visible; they must have been smoothed down or pressed out while
the paint was still fresh. Along certain axes, often at the righthand limit

82. Piero della Francesca, *Constantine and His Army* (detail).
Arezzo, S. Francesco.

83. Giotto and assistants, Detail of a border. Padua, Arena Chapel.
Polished *secco su fresco*.

of the surface, a line of very small drops of paint is visible. The vehicle
seems to have contained a kind of saponified oil, and the iron that was
employed to press the damp paint must have been hot.

If traditional words are used to describe this technique, it can only
be classified by the paradoxical term *secco su fresco*. Thus both groups
of students of Roman mural technique were, to a degree, right, at least
with regard to monochromatic surfaces. The vehicle is the one normally
associated in the past with secco, while the condition of the intonaco is
characteristic of fresco. Along with *buon fresco* this technique was
employed shortly after 1300. We are tempted to say revived, but the
present state of knowledge of mediaeval mural practices does not permit a generalization of this kind. Giotto used *secco su fresco* in the
Arena Chapel for the depiction of marble. He painted in this manner
all the marble panels in the decorative bands (Fig. 83), the twenty-
eight marble panels that, with the Vices and Virtues, compose the
base, and seven structures within the scenes: the base of the throne
of God on the triumphal arch, the wall of the temple in the *Expulsion of Joachim* (Fig. 79) and in the *Presentation of the Virgin*, the
panels of the balcony in the *Massacre of the Innocents*, the lid of
the sarcophagus in the *Raising of Lazarus*, the tomb in the *Noli Me
Tangere*, and the pavement in *Inconstancy*.

These surfaces in the Arena Chapel are identifiable by the same physical qualities that distinguish the *secco su fresco* at Pompeii. The strokes of the brush have been ironed out, and the surface, without the irregularity and roughness of *buon fresco* and *secco*, is flat and smooth as a mirror. Small beads are again visible at the end of the passage of the iron, and in places one can even see the horizontal lines between two strokes of the iron. The technique, far from showing the relative weakness of secco, proved more durable than fresco. In numerous instances in the Chapel the ironed *secco su fresco* used for marble has resisted moisture whereas the fresco immediately around it has deteriorated (Fig. 83).

It is notable that Giotto, like the ancient Romans, matched his technique to his representation, developing a sort of visual onomatopoeia. His simulated marble was smooth, polished, and brilliant like the real article itself. And the ironing may well have added to the counterfeited random diffusion of color in the veins an element of real accident or chance. We have not identified similar surfaces in post-Giottesque murals, but we have not been close enough to many of them for sound judgment. The *secco su fresco* technique is, however, still employed in Italy today for the painting of simulated marble. In Tuscany it is called *stucco romano*.

The recognition of the employment of secco by Giotto in the Peruzzi Chapel and of *secco su fresco* in antiquity and in the Arena Chapel led us to watch for other variants from the commonly expected techniques in fourteenth and fifteenth century mural painting. The "frescoes" that are more beautiful in color than any others provide a notable instance. The paintings by Piero della Francesca in the choir at Arezzo present a design of intonaco patches that at first seems to be characteristic of *buon fresco*. The patches are large in the skies and much smaller in the areas of the figures (Figs. 80, 82). Often each figure, or at least each part of a figure that bears one color, is allotted a patch. The painter, however, departs from this normal fresco practice with exceptional frequency. He seldom, moreover, isolated a head, the execution of which required a disproportionate amount of time.

Earlier painters when working in fresco avoided executing a coloristically continuous area on two patches of intonaco. Paint applied to plaster with water as a vehicle dries a different color, and when, because of a change in the design, an area had to be completed on a second patch the added surface does not quite match. Piero, however, while obviously wishing to work on damp intonaco, cared much less about the precise coincidence of a patch with an area of color, and he permitted one area of color to fall into two or three patches. The torso of Maxentius was painted on two patches (Fig. 81), and so was the soldier behind Constantine wearing highly reflective plate armor— a very complex surface (Fig. 82). The right arm of the shrieking figure in the *Death of Adam* falls onto two patches, as does the body of Adam (Fig. 80). In each of these instances the colors match across the boundary of the patch. Sometimes the brushstrokes even carry across the joints, from one patch that was still damp to one that had dried.

What is the explanation of these procedures? Piero's colors apparently changed less as they dried. Much of his paint, moreover, is bright and luminous, without the characteristic dryness of *buon fresco*. The paint film seems to possess the thickness of tempera. The surfaces to which we refer were not however executed *a secco;* where Piero employed this traditional technique in the choir, as for the leaves of the great tree in the *Death of Adam,* the usual deterioration has occurred. The division into patches definitely implies a wish to paint on damp plaster. Piero must have employed *secco su fresco*—without, however, pressing the paint film. The technique would have offered advantages beyond a greater luminosity. Very important to a master concerned with such surfaces as armor would have been the less rapid drying of the paint. Perhaps too *secco su fresco* permitted a wider range of pigments than *buon fresco*—certainly the range of color of the Arezzo frescoes was not earlier achieved in fresco.

Certainty about Piero's technique can be obtained only by a skilful chemical analysis. If we have drawn the correct inference from the physical characteristics we may add that the coloristic effects desired by Piero and his contemporaries motivated the development of a novel technique—novel, yet, as we have seen, not without important precedents. Recently Giovanni Paccagnini has suggested that in the Camera degli Sposi Mantegna did not work in *buon fresco*, though in some places at least the *giornate* of this technique are visible.[4] The paint is thick and dense, rather like Piero's. We shall not be surprised if the use of *secco su fresco* proves to have been not uncommon in the middle and late Quattrocento. The technique offered the painter not only a great range and richness of color but a partial escape from fresco's tyranny of speed and time.

NOTES

1. Some of the observations recorded in the present appendix were presented by L. Tintori (and amplified by M. Meiss) at a symposium on the conservation of mural paintings held at the Institute of Fine Arts of New York University in October 1962, under the auspices of the Conservation Center.

2. Above, p. 6 and n. 6. M. Cagiano de Azevedo, writing from his extensive experience in the Istituto Centrale del Restauro in Rome, has stated that much of Etruscan mural painting has proved to be fresco (*Enciclopedia dell'arte antica*, Rome, 1958, s.v. "Affresco").

3. In our reference to this house in 1962 (p. 6) we designated it, following local usage, *Casa dello Scheletro*. See K. Schefold, *Die Wände Pompejis*, Berlin, 1957, pp. 22ff. V. Spinazzola, *Pompei*, Rome, 1953, figs. 608ff., calls it *Casa del Criptoportico*.

4. "Appunti sulla tecnica della 'camera picta' di Andrea Mantegna," in *Scritti di storia dell'arte in onore di Mario Salmi*, Rome, 1962, II, pp. 395–403.

INDEX

The Appendix of 1964 has not been indexed.

Norton Library titles in

Art, Architecture and the Philosophy of Art